Room to Grow

ALSO BY CHRISTINA BAKER KLINE

Desire Lines

Sweet Water

Child of Mine:
Original Essays on Becoming a Mother (editor)

The Conversation Begins:
Mothers and Daughters Talk About Living Feminism
(with Christina L. Baker)

Room to Grow

Twenty-two writers encounter the pleasures and paradoxes of raising young children

CHRISTINA BAKER KLINE

editor

Golden Books

NEW YORK

Golden Books®

888 Seventh Avenue
New York, NY 10106

An excerpt from "Looking Back at Night" by David Whyte.
Reprinted by permission of David Whyte and Many Rivers
Press. "Uprooting the Kids" by Francine Prose. Copyright
© 1987 by Francine Prose. Reprinted by permission
of George Borchardt, Inc. Originally appeared in
Working Mother magazine.

Designed by Gwen Petruska Gürkan

Manufactured in the United States of America

10 9 8 7 6 5 4 3 2 1

Library of Congress Cataloging-in-Publication Data

Room to grow : 22 writers encounter the pleasures and
paradoxes of raising young children /
    Christina Baker Kline, editor.
        ISBN 1-58238-032-5 (alk. paper)
        1. Parenting.   2. Child rearing.   3. Parents—
Attitudes.   I. Kline, Christina Baker, 1964—   .
    HQ755.8.R66   1999
    649'.1—dc21   98-56270
                                                            CIP

To Cynthia,

sister, mother, friend

Now, by the small body of my sleeping son
the hidden river in my chest flows with my son's
and I time my speech to the rhythm of his breath

joining my night with his, singing his night song
as if those waters underground
were secret rivers washing through the soul

bringing out the untold life
which is the stream he'll join in growing old,
in silent hours when his sureness

of his self recedes. There he'll find
the rest between the solid notes
that makes the song worthwhile.

David Whyte,
from "Looking Back at Night,"
Where Many Rivers Meet

CONTENTS

INTRODUCTION

*T*his book began as a way for me to make sense of the toddler years.
I have never been able to make sense of things in the usual way, like reading advice books and how-to guides. I tend to find meaning instead in art
and drama, through storytelling and metaphor. So when my two boys,
Hayden and Will, seventeen months apart, emerged from babyhood into
something more complicated and less defined, I began looking for stories
that would help to explain my own shifting feelings and changing experience.

A sizable body of literature exists on parenting young children.
Much of it is intended for reassurance: More than likely, your child is
perfectly normal; children change rapidly as they grow; we parents do
the best we can. Or it offers advice: Limit television, encourage creativity. Don't overreact to small crises. Read to your child. A good deal of
this information is useful, and much of it is valid. But as I made my way
through books and magazines with growing impatience, I realized that I
didn't particularly want to be instructed. I was looking for something
deeper and more profound—a metaphysical guide to parenting.

Three years ago, when Hayden was a baby, I edited a collection of
thirty original essays on becoming a mother, *Child of Mine*. I asked my
contributors—Mona Simpson, Susan Cheever, Allegra Goodman, Naomi
Wolf, Meg Wolitzer, and Valerie Sayers, among others—to write candidly
about the first year of motherhood, an overwhelming, joyful, and often
traumatic time. I wanted them to focus on the details of their personal
experience, centered around a specific issue. As Hayden metamorphosed

from a baby to a child, I began to envision a new collection that would be an extension of the conversation about raising children that was begun in that first book. This new collection, as I imagined it, would be broader in scope and focus. It would draw on the experiences of men as well as women, and its emphasis would shift from the parent to the child.

No other phase of a child's development rivals the first year for sheer intensity. But as babies become children and their personalities begin to emerge, the focus changes from our experience to theirs: their interests and desires, their development, who they are becoming. For that reason I knew it would be constrictive to limit the scope of discussion in *Room to Grow* to a few years. Contributors would need room to go back and forth, explore recurring questions and evolving perspectives. Each new age and stage sheds light on the previous one; sometimes it takes years for patterns to emerge and stories to unfold. So in the end I encouraged contributors to expand their discussion from one particular aspect of their experience to a larger view. I set some parameters—the pieces would center on children between the ages of about two and ten, the period when our children are young and wholly dependent, before they have begun to actively differentiate. And I gave contributors a list of potential topics to use as catalysts for discussion, ranging from specific subjects like religion, sibling rivalry, and potty training, to more impressionistic ones like imagination and seeing yourself in your child.

Room to Grow evolved over the course of a year. I asked equal numbers of men and women to contribute, from a wide spectrum of ages, experience, writing styles, geographical locations, and cultural and ethnic backgrounds. As well as approaching writers whose work I knew and admired, I sought out some who may be lesser known, reasoning that a fresh perspective often comes from an unexpected source. The final list is largely self-selecting: Just over a third are men, with a near-equal balance of fiction and nonfiction writers (indeed, many contributors do both), memoirists, poets, and journalists, specialists in humor, mystery, and feature writing. The age range spans more than thirty years; contributors are scattered across the country, from Maine to Mississippi, New York to California, Vermont to Montana.

I asked contributors to be both intensely personal and self-analytical, two perhaps conflicting requests. I wanted the essays to be revealing and honest—risky in some way. I sought a balance of humor and pathos, intensity and lightness. In some cases I found myself asking writers to compromise their artistic standards by explaining more than they wanted to, and in others I pushed people to explore raw, painful, or uncomfortable material, beyond what might have felt safe. I found that fiction writers were sometimes uncomfortable stepping back from their stories to analyze their own experience, preferring to let the story speak for itself. Journalists, on the other hand, were occasionally tempted to use familiar hooks and other devices to move their essays along. I sometimes had to nudge them to go beyond that genre's style formulas of anecdote and solution, and delve into less familiar territory.

In asking men to contribute, I wanted them to address the very issues that often exclude them from the discussion to begin with. For example, how do fathers model behavior for their young children? How do they deal with the issue of discipline? Gender? Balancing work and parenting? Creating an egalitarian home? To my surprise I found that despite their different styles and subjects, a number of first drafts by men shared a common trait: While mothers often spoke about the complications of dealing with the outside world's perceptions of one's child, highlighting moments of conflict or vulnerability, fathers were more likely to share witty, clever, or insightful comments their kids had made or precocious things they had done. One father's first draft included an entire page, punctuated with bullet points, of these kinds of moments. "I marvel at everything my daughter does," he explained a little sheepishly when I suggested that the list may be more appropriate for a personal scrapbook than an essay. "I forget that every parent experiences such moments. I tend to think they're unique to my child."

In the end, the pieces in this book are candid, reflective, and intimate. Telling stories small and large, exploring the "whys" rather than the "how-to's" of raising children, these essayists capture the essence of parenthood: what it means to be deeply connected to another human being, and then what we face as we begin the attenuated process of letting go.

*   *   *

When we have children, we give up autonomy; we may sacrifice or redefine careers; we make decisions based on their welfare instead of our own. No matter what we do, we are haunted by the sense that we're not doing enough, giving enough. And we come to understand that our children will always consume the available space, whatever that space is. What we gain in exchange is a deeper, richer understanding of what life means. In some ways it is a Faustian bargain; we may feel that we have given up ourselves. Once you have children, you are never alone. Even when they're not with you, they are a part of you, their presence as acutely felt as a phantom limb.

Room to Grow is about many things, the most pervasive being how we as parents cope with this dual gift and burden. "I think it is true that nowhere are we as crazy as we are with our own children," writes contributor Susan Fromberg Schaeffer. "They call on such deep things in us. They are us, and yet they are not us." Roberta Israeloff, in an essay on navigating a relationship with an adolescent son, writes, "Children, if you listen to them closely, give you a window on your own soul, your own deepest chaotic illogical desires. . . . Having children is the most illuminating and subversive act I have ever perpetuated."

This collection is divided into three sections—"Conjuring a Family," "Room to Grow," and "Taking Wing," which borrows its title from the moving piece by Larry Brown that ends the book. Arranged in rough chronological order, the essays range from pieces about very young children to a number that explore, in different ways, the transition from childhood into adolescence. Some pieces, ruminative and far-reaching, span the full first decade of a child's life. Contributors to this book probe questions that lie at the core of modern parenthood: How do you raise children with religion when you yourself are ambivalent? Might the names we choose for our children end up affecting the way we feel about them? How can we reconcile our Utopian vision for our children's lives with the sometimes harsh realities they face? What do our children have to teach us about the way we measure time? How do you learn to parent a child if you yourself never had a childhood? Some writers use seemingly ordinary moments—the after-school carpool, an embarrassing incident at school, the ritual of bedtime stories, soccer practice—to illuminate larger issues about connection and identity. In a few cases the essays indirectly complement each other: a story about being a stay-at-home father contrasts with one on guilt and the working mother; a piece on parenting one child is balanced by another on creating a family out of a disparate mix of ethnicities and backgrounds.

Introduction

Ultimately, the stories in this collection tell us about ourselves, shedding light on dark corners of our experience, articulating for us things we hope and fear but haven't known how to express. For me, this project has been—among other things—a process of coming to terms with my own ambivalence about letting go. Sooner or later we have to give our children up to their own lives. How we learn to do this and what it means lie at the heart of this book.

PART I

ONJURING A FAMILY

On Naming a Child

SUSAN FROMBERG SCHAEFFER

I remember everything about the day we brought home our first child—everything except the weather. Already the world seemed to have contracted around us, a flexible, transparent bubble in which my husband and I and our son were sealed. And in this new, smaller globe of ours, the weather was determined by our son. If he was healthy and not running a temperature, our weather was fine, but if he was ill or feverish, we had dismal weather. It was as if our world had suddenly been conquered and was now being ruled by a very small god.

Our son was named Benjamin—after my grandfather, the great love of my childhood. I went everywhere with my grandfather. In a family that appeared to disapprove of the very existence of females, he preferred them. When my brother arrived, my grandfather alone was not stunned with delight, and our outings went on as before.

Fortunately, Benjamin the child took after his namesake. He had the same blue eyes and blond hair, and, as it turned out, the same tempera-ment, which was also my temperament. There must have been uncount-able times during each day of his infancy when I looked at him and thought—but *thought* is not the right word—believed, without knowing I believed, that I had my grandfather back. The child had somehow re-trieved one of the two most important people of my childhood, one of the two people now lost to me, people I could not recover, not even in dreams. I was ecstatic—if ecstatic is a delirious enough word to describe how I felt—as if a stone wall of the universe, hidden behind the sky, had opened and let one of my magic beings come through.

But what works once does not always work twice. When my daughter was born, we named her after my grandmother, May Levine. My grandmother had lived with us when I was a child. She had long silver hair that hung down her back in a braid, and the tip of the braid was brown. At night, when my parents slept, I would take my pillow and creep through the hall, and when I reached the foot of her bed, I would slowly crawl up toward the head of the bed and then settle in for the night. My mother tried to stop this, but she would fall asleep first, and so in the morning I was always discovered in bed with my grandmother.

She fought with everyone. She fought with my grandfather, who in turn had menaced her with a gun. She chased my father around the kitchen because he had threatened to hit me. She fought with me because I did not make my bed on time and was "killing my mother." She was a creature of high drama made up of lowly details like unmade beds or unswept floors or stained dresses, and she loved me. Even when I came home from college, she would see me and begin to cry with happiness. Someone who loves you as desperately as my grandmother loved me means everything to you. And so I named my daughter after my grandmother: May. It seemed a simple and natural thing to do. You celebrate the person who is gone by bestowing her name on a new being. That should be all there is to it.

Of course, there is a restriction. If you are Jewish, you are not to name a child after a person who is still living. I have asked for explanations of this and received many. Among other things, I have been told it is bad luck to name a child after someone still alive; the gods or the fates may decide two such people aren't needed, and doom the older one. The child may disgrace her namesake, or vice versa. I have never heard an explanation that quite satisfied me, but this is not the point. The fact of the prohibition—do not name a child after a living person—points to psychological complexities involved in the naming process, and I was to become aware of many of them after the birth of my daughter.

Unlike her brother, May was not a quiet baby. She often woke during the night, crying inconsolably, and calmed only by my talking to her and touching her. Because she would often begin to cry ten minutes after she had been put back in her crib, I took to lying on the floor, half beneath her crib. Then when she cried, I would reach up with my hand and feel for her knee or her foot or her hand, and she would become quiet. I grew quite used to sleeping on the floor. May was beautiful, if bald, and she and I seemed well on our way to becoming that strange beast, half-mother, half-child.

I adored her. But there were moments when I looked at her and felt an odd annoyance, as if she had just done something to disappoint me, and because I could find no explanation for what seemed to me an utterly aberrant response, I was increasingly disturbed by my own reactions.

And then, as she grew, I began to have more trouble with her. For no reason, I would find myself looking at her bald head, and I would begin to feel the already all-too familiar annoyance and then real anger. "She's bald!" I said to my mother. My mother said, "Don't worry. No child ever starts kindergarten with a bald head." Later, I complained because she didn't talk. "When can she talk?" my mother asked me. "Your son is always talking."

I wondered if what was wrong with me was what other people recognized as postpartum depression, but when I went to a psychoanalyst, he said that was not my problem. *My problem.* If it was not postpartum depression, then I was like a wild animal who rejected one of her young. There was no reason for it, and nothing could be done about it; nothing could stop it.

I do not mean to say here that I was always angry at May, but I was often angry, often incapable of feeling sympathy, often outraged, as if she had done something or failed to do something. But what could a six-month-old-child or a one-year-old child or a two- or three-year-old child possibly have done? My responses were incommensurate with anything in reality. As time passed, they grew weaker, and then without warning they would suddenly *come back,* and I would once more feel as if I had taken leave of my senses.

It is hard to summon up now the feeling of looniness, of sheer craziness, of desperate, trapped unhappiness that all this awakened in me. It is painful to remember the hours I spent asking myself again and again if I was meant to be a mother, if I should ever have had children in the first place. Like every other woman I've ever known, I had sworn I would not make the mistakes with my children that my mother had made with me, but now it seemed likely that I would be (although once I would have believed such a thing absolutely impossible) a *worse* mother than my own mother was. It is ghastly to remember how I cried against my husband's chest and said I was not a good mother and would ruin my child, to remember the calculations I made even as I cried: How much of this can you tell him before he begins to wonder if you really are a bad mother? *Before he begins to think twice and wants to get rid of you?* But he was the only person to whom I could speak. I could not speak to my own mother. I do not think we had a single conversation about anything personal when I was growing up, although my mother often held forth eloquently on the virtues of Clorox or of taking a few things up the steps each time you went from the first floor to the second: "That way," she said, "you won't find yourself with a big job at the end of the day." I had talked to my grandmother, or, rather, my grandmother had talked to me. She told me about her troubles with my grandfather; she took me to visit her friends, and afterward told me stories of their lives. But my mother was silent—except on the subject of housecleaning. And when she broke her silence, it was to be condemnatory. Nothing I did pleased her. Everything I did would lead to disaster. When I looked down at my daughter and felt inexplicable anger, almost rage, I began to believe my mother. I was worthless as a human being. I had failed as a mother.

And everywhere, other new mothers had new daughters and cooed their names happily and were not dissatisfied—or so it seemed to me. But now I wonder: How many other people made the same mistake and gave the child a name they thought they could live with, only to have given the child an ability to reach deep wells of bitterness, layers of mystery that should long ago have become unreachable, locked?

I had come to believe that May, who was almost three and would not or could not talk, was a stupid child and that it was too bad she was, because it was my opinion that intelligent people made their way more easily through life. When it was time for her to go to kindergarten, the schools had a new rule. Children could attend school for only a half day unless they passed the test for gifted children. "Don't bother taking her," I told my husband. "It will only upset her when she fails, and you'll waste your time." He was taking her all the same, he said. I was stunned by the sheer folly of this and refused to hear more about it. I dressed May, gave her a cookie, and sent her off to be humiliated.

The next morning, the phone rang, and a voice said, "Mrs. Schaeffer, your daughter has passed the test for the gifted children's program."

"Oh," I said, "there must be a mistake. You don't mean May Schaeffer?"

I could hear the woman rustling her papers. "Yes," she said, "May Schaeffer. She passed the test. Her math scores are very high."

"Please look again," I asked her. "You must have the wrong child."

"Mrs. Schaeffer," the woman said, her patience fraying, "your child was the *only* child who took the test yesterday."

My husband found me sitting on the edge of our bed. He asked me what happened. I said that May had passed the test. "I knew it," he said. He wanted to know what I was so gloomy about. Wouldn't he be gloomy, I asked him, if he'd made such a terrible miscalculation about one of his own children?

In a way it was true that if May had passed the test, then I had failed a test of my own. How could I have so underestimated her? I rarely underestimate anyone. Among friends I have a reputation for uncanniness; I know what a person is like and what is likely to become of them. How had I gone so wrong here? I began to think back, and when I did, I remembered one particular night when I was sitting with May in my lap, stroking her still hairless head, and repeating her name over and over: *May, May, May,* and then *Maisie, Maisie, Maisie,* which was one of my nicknames for her, as it had been one of my grandmother's nicknames, and for no reason whatever I began to cry. Where *was* May, the May I wanted? This little thing in my lap had not replaced her but only summoned her up each time I called her by my grandmother's name, because that was the trouble—*May* was still my grandmother's name. The existence of a child named May, who was not *May,* who did not resemble her volatile grandmother in the least, who resembled no one in the family because she was

14

so calm in her very genes, who even as a small infant possessed a wonderful inner gyroscope—the existence of this child named May proved a torment to me. Each time I called her name, I was not calling her; I was calling my grandmother. Each time the child responded, the response could not satisfy me—the child could not become the lost person.

In those days I kept a journal, and in it I complained that I never dreamed about the people I loved who had died; it seemed cruel that even in my dreams I could not have them back. I knew many people who complained about their dead parents or grandparents who haunted their dreams. But my dead were recalcitrant. In life they had been hard realists. Dead was dead. They were above making cameo appearances in dreams.

I think now that when I named my son after his grandfather, I had finished mourning my grandfather. I think now that when I named my daughter after my grandmother, I had not yet begun to mourn her. I was not ready for a child named May, a child who would constantly remind me of what I had lost. I had no idea that in the act of naming my daughter, I was creating a being whom I would come to resent.

I do not mean to imply that any of this was conscious. If it had been, it would never have gone on so long. Like many women, I tend to feel guilty about everything—I've done this wrong, I haven't done that, I should have done whatever it was more often or less often—and I was particularly vulnerable to guilt when it came to my children. If I had known what I had done by giving my daughter a dangerous name, I would have managed, somehow, to change. Certainly I could have changed her name or called her by a different one. "Stop the nonsense!" my mother would have said, and I would have stopped the nonsense. But it took me a long time to understand what had happened—and I blame myself still because any time that passes while a mother is reacting badly to a child is too long a time. I do not mean to say, either, that this—what can I call it? this nuttiness—went on incessantly. Most of the time I adored my child. But in the end it was the passage of time that cured me. I would like to say it was time that cured *us*, but I am still afraid that I caused damage during those years of calling *May, May, May* when I was calling out for my grandmother and not my daughter.

I was lucky; we were lucky. Time passed, and the child May became herself, became unmistakably herself, a remarkable, altogether unexpected aberration in an introspective family who volunteered to go on what seemed to me thousand-mile walks for charity, who taught herself the violin so that she could play in the school orchestra, who could work out math problems by looking into the air as she thought and then writing down the answer. I remember once having terrible trouble writing a novel I was sure I would never finish, and I thought I had given up on it. That winter my daughter had bronchitis, as she did almost every winter. She lay on a couch watching the Olympics, which fascinated her but ordinarily would have bored me to death. I crept onto the couch with her. She told me to get off. I kept creeping back on until she let me stay there. I lay on that couch with my head on her hip for two weeks, and at the end of those two weeks, the Olympics were over, and I got up, went upstairs, and started working on the impossible novel, which had suddenly become possible. I had been cured by those two weeks on the couch—by *this* May, not *that* May.

I had crept into bed with both Mays, but my grandmother would not have been comforting if she had known I had a task I was not able to finish. She would have shouted at me and tried to frighten me into working. She would have said, "You'll end up selling ribbons in Macy's!" May, my daughter, said nothing. She kept me company. She was thirteen and did not want her mother around, but she made an allowance for me. She must have taken a look at my face and made her calculations. She must have decided that it was more important for me to stay than for her to send me away. She was generous-hearted and intuitive. She was not, in fact, like her grandmother at all.

Later, when I had finished the novel that had once seemed impossible, my agent called to say she needed another copy by four the next afternoon. At that time I had a printer that took longer to print out a manuscript than it took me to write it. I got up early in the morning and began printing. When May came home from school at three-thirty, she saw how far I had gotten and calculated that at the rate I was going, I might finish by three in the morning. She volunteered to stay in the room and watch the printer, which meant that I could leave, at least for ten or fifteen minutes at a time. But around eleven at night, I said, "I don't think I can do it. I'm going to bed." May looked at me and said, "You can do it, Ma. I'll stay up here and help you." I fell asleep for half an hour, and when I got up, I tried to send her to bed, but she would not leave—not until she saw I was finished.

Something had happened. A door had blown open. May, who had become more open and more cooperative, had also become more rebellious. She began to ask me to write poems for her when she had to hand poems in to class. Before she asked me to do this, I was never sure she *knew* that I wrote, so thoroughly did she manage to ignore me when it suited her. She suddenly asked me to type her papers and to proofread them, and she accepted criticism without screaming. Peace and quiet were not restored; quite the opposite. Perhaps there had always been, until then, too much peace and quiet between us. Now we began to argue. I asked her, Did *everything* she wore have to be either gray or black?

What was wrong with wearing lipstick? *Why* did her hair have to cover her eyes? *Why* did she think that green dye would wash out? And then I broke my own rule about not commenting on boyfriends. "What are you doing with him?" I asked her.

"I don't know," she said. "I'm thinking of breaking up."

Never one to let well enough alone, I asked her, "What did you go out with him for in the first place?"

"I was desperate," she said.

The blunt honesty of the answer, the humility of it, humbled me. I would never have been capable of answering my own mother, or anyone else, in that way.

That settled it. Wherever my grandmother was, she was not in that room, not then and not later.

I have told this story because I believe that there is nothing we know so little about as how we are raising our own child. Our children come to us as the proverbial tabula rasa, the blank page, and we know we have to teach them about their world and about what is right and wrong, and we assume that when we speak, we know what we are saying and why. But often we are saying what my mother always said, although never with words: *Be like me. Be me!* I did not want my daughter to be like me—I had a dim enough view of my own character to strangle such a wish in its bed—but still I wanted her to be like someone else. I wanted her to *be* someone else.

I think it is true that nowhere are we as crazy as we are with our own children. They call on such deep things in us. They are us, and yet they are not us. We are young, and they are as young as it is possible for any human to be. They are, when they first arrive, of an age we cannot ever remember having been ourselves, and so they are magic and so they are mysterious. I now think that naming a child is like giving a title to a painting before you have picked up the brush or touched the canvas. The very act of naming has already painted in the outlines of a picture. If the canvas resists the painter and the painting fights to become something we did not intend it to be, we are confused and sometimes angry.

In almost every case, whatever name we give our child will immediately become *his* or *her* name and will not be an emblem of someone else. Yet, even as I write this, I am still shocked by how little I knew what I was doing when I gave my daughter her name, and if this in-the-darkness can be true of naming a child, then it can also be true of an infinite number of decisions we make—all of which, at the time, seem more than rational; they seem the sensible, absolutely right and proper thing. And it seems to me now that our real relations with our children take place somewhere in the blood-dark, somewhere beneath the earth, and we speak to them in our own voices, and in the voices of small animals who live beneath the earth and large animals who hunt above it, somewhere where we ourselves are still children, where we all grope and float toward one another as part of the vast horde of the unborn.

Our children are becoming themselves as we are still becoming what we are. Our confrontations with them are often not mere disputes but full-blown wars. And perhaps this is how it has to be. We fight with our children as if our lives and theirs depended on it. And in a deeper sense, they do.

When I think about naming my daughter, I realize that any normal process can be distorted, and all I can say to others is what we always say: Take care. We are playing with our children, but immense forces are playing with us. It *is* a miracle, as my mother used to say, that any of us grow up. It is odd to be writing this now, in the shadow of my daughter's wedding. And I mean to use the word *shadow* in both its senses. The shadow is a darkness, an absence of light. Who knows what will happen to my daughter after she marries? I do not envy a son-in-law who mistreats her. I am, after all, my grandmother's grandchild, and my grandmother chased my father with a knife when he tried to hit me. But my daughter seems to have picked well. And a shadow is more than a darkness; it is a shelter against what can be the terrible heat of the sun. I hope someday to be such a shelter for her: May, my daughter; May, the name of my daughter.

The Education of a
Stay-at-Home Father

MICHAEL LASER

*M*y daughter is screaming.

The other children all have on their sky-blue nursery school T-shirts, but Helen—for no reason that I or her teachers can discern—refuses to wear hers. "You have to put on the blue shirt so you won't get lost at the amusement park," I tell her (thinking, *Why* must she wear the damn shirt if I'm going to be with her the whole time? And why, out of all these kids, must mine be the only one throwing a tantrum?), but her response is to drop to the floor and writhe while the other children and teachers and class mothers watch her and watch me, the only father in sight, the one parent who can't handle his child. It doesn't matter that she's cheerful and cooperative most of the time; right now she's acting like a beast with her foot in a steel trap, and I have no idea what to do. In the end I carry her—straining against me, still screaming even though I've stuffed the blue T-shirt into her diaper bag—onto the yellow bus and down the narrow aisle, holding her feet so she won't kick anyone in the head. The bus rumbles and roars, we bounce through the neighboring towns, and Helen's inexplicable rage slowly abates, as it always does.

At the amusement park she rides the merry-go-round four times, and we take the train together three times, and I watch her grip the little steering wheel of the pink boat as it goes around and around in its circular pool, her smile of pleasure compressed slightly by self-consciousness because she feels me watching: my heart aching with adoration for my beautiful girl, this smooth, round-faced little person who is no longer a baby but her own willful, incomprehensible self.

This is a story of misery and joy.

*　　*　　*

I never wanted a job. I'm a writer; every job I've ever held has felt like a theft of my time. And so, when my wife's maternity leave ended, we agreed that I would stay home with our three-month-old daughter. Jennifer would commute to the city and bring back the money, since she earned more than I ever had and actually derived satisfaction from her work. I, meanwhile, would rock Helen on my shoulder when she cried, mix the Enfamil, and write during her naps.

The arrangement made perfect sense—but I hadn't anticipated the terror or the boredom. Each morning, as I woke and remembered that I would be responsible all day for this vulnerable, alien creature who depended on me entirely and couldn't speak, I would cover my head with a pillow for as long as possible, paralyzed with fear. We had just moved from Manhattan to Montclair, New Jersey; for living space, broad-aisled supermarkets, and a car, we had traded in the buzz and dazzle of the city I loved. Condemned to solitary confinement and sensory deprivation, I took Helen out for long walks in the snow, hoping to see other people—a Manhattan habit pathetically unsuited to the suburbs. The wheels of her carriage barely fit through the narrow shoveled paths, and caught constantly on slate sidewalk slabs that had been lifted by tree roots. Just as mothers forget the pain of childbirth, I can't remember how I got through those first few months.

The loneliness eased once she began to speak—but other anxieties remained. Like the President of the United States, I had to live with the knowledge that the smallest of my actions would have consequences. The way I talked to Helen now, and how I dealt with our conflicts, would create happiness or neurosis in her future. If I continued to say *don't* as often as I did—"Don't walk in that mud," "Don't put your hand so close to that candle," "Don't fling those tax papers in the air"—a little cop might grow inside her head who blew his whistle each time she got ready to do anything remotely adventurous. I tried to censor myself, to let her get dirty, explore, and make minor mischief, but more often than not, my need for order overpowered my good intentions.

There was another, less comical anxiety lurking behind the others. What if a child needs to be with its mother, or at least with a woman, in order to grow up whole? I mentioned this concern to a few friends, most of them women, and they all (being friends) assured me that I was a great father, that Helen was lucky to have me at home, and so forth. The question remained, though: *Will she get what she needs from me?*

* * *

My ambition to be a writer has always involved visions of glory. From college on, I worked hard, confident that I would amaze the world by my thirtieth birthday, soaring above friends who became mere doctors and lawyers.

It didn't happen that way. After twenty years of hard labor, I find myself more or less anonymous. No prizes, no fame, no money—just a bunch of stories in literary magazines, a children's picture book, and a novel to be published by a small press. Instead of smiling in the sun of universal adulation, I lack even the normal respectability of a job.

And how do I spend my days? At home with a three-year-old, making a few thousand dollars a year from freelance writing while my wife earns four-fifths of our money.

There are two things to say about this. First, many women who give up work to stay home with their children report the same discomfort. In this country, if you don't earn your own money, no matter how worthwhile your reasons, you end up feeling small and embarrassed. Second, for a father especially, earning little or nothing means walking around in a permanent haze of shame.

Fortunately for me, my wife is less scornful than grateful, because our daughter (unlike many) has a parent at home during the day. I consider it a testament to Jennifer's character that she doesn't disdain me for doing what most people, in their heart of hearts, consider a woman's job. Among friends and family, though, I suspect I'm viewed as a nice guy who has failed. Men friends never ask about or comment on my situation—the Code forbids it—but I imagine they would rather work in a salt mine than trade places with me. And my elderly neighbors, most of them born in Italy, must see me pushing Helen in her stroller when other men are working and wonder, *Che cosa fa?* What's this guy doing?

When I'm with Helen, though (that is, for most of my waking hours), there is little room to brood over injuries to my pride. Our days are a stew of errands, sudden rages, and unexpected joys. The reality of the work preempts self-pity.

Underlying everything is exhaustion. She wakes each day before seven, hours before I would like her to. We hear her thundering feet coming our way, and I hide under the covers. Climbing into bed between us, she tells Jennifer about a dream or about a toy she covets. Then, on weekdays at least, I drag myself out of bed and help her choose her clothes for the day.

My yearning for sleep makes me dull company on these weekday mornings. The moment we get downstairs, Helen says, "I want to watch." I'm only too happy to turn on *Sesame Street* or a Disney video so I can dress her while she's too mesmerized to impishly put her legs into her shirtsleeves. Even in my drowsiness, though, when she climbs onto my lap for socks and shoes, I can't resist tickling her and making her wiggle and laugh.

You never know whether the morning will go smoothly or horrifically. When the pediatrician changed her vitamin dosage and the new pills turned out to be square instead of round, we had fights every day for weeks because she refused to take them. I would stand between her and the television, blocking her view of Barney and insisting, "They're the same vitamin! It's just a different shape!" and she would do her best to ignore me. One day she said dismissively, "Would you go in the kitchen?"— a teenager, ten years early.

While she's neutralized by the TV, I dress, shave, make her lunch for school, and fortify myself for the inevitable struggle over . . . turning off the TV.

Simply saying, "Okay, time to turn it off," would produce a tantrum, so first I warn her: "In five minutes we're going to turn this off and eat breakfast." Then I come over and put her on my lap, giving her the remote control. "After this skit," I forewarn her. When the scene is ending, I say, "Now," and she says, "Not yet!" and I say, "If you don't turn it off, I

will." Here she will usually hand the control back and say, "You do it"—
except on the days when she goes berserk.

I don't understand what causes her tantrums, but I do know they
usually come when she hasn't eaten in hours or is overtired. Crabby and
antagonistic, she fixes on something she can't have—a video that we've
already returned to the library, or Cocoa Puffs for lunch—and when I say
no, she whines, then demands, then screams. I can't count the number of
times I've carried her howling to her room or to the car or out of a
restaurant. Lately, as the intervals between tantrums have grown longer
and I've come to expect more or less reasonable behavior from her, I find
that her sudden eruptions of contrariness provoke my anger almost instantly. *"Don't do this!"* I snap. It never helps.

While Helen is in school, I race to cram three careers into three and
a half hours: writing fiction, writing grant proposals for pay, and fixing
anything that has broken in the house (or planting flowers, mowing the
lawn, etc.). Having stolen this bit of time to do the work I care about,
plus the work that earns me money (and therefore the right to hold my
head up), plus the household tasks that gnaw at me if left undone, I'm
happier than at any other time of the day and look forward to seeing her
again.

When I pick her up from school, she comes running at the sight of
me, calling, "Daddyyyyyyy!" and banging into my crouching embrace.
She's been doing this since her first days in nursery school; it's just a ritual by now, but it still lifts my soul every time.

We rarely leave school right away because Helen usually wants to
run around the lobby or the front lawn with her friends. She especially
likes playing with boys—the rougher the better. She dives into the snow
with them, flops down on top of them, and shrieks exuberantly. It's good

to see her from this distance once in a while—to remember, after our battles, that she's only three feet tall.

After lunch, Helen goes upstairs with me. I draw the shades in her room and read books to her while she eats one last snack. (She can never seem to eat a full meal in one sitting. If I don't give her a snack, hunger will keep her from napping.) On cold winter days she nestles against me and looks at the pictures, and then the welcome warmth of her body becomes a reflection of the love she draws out of me. These are some of our best times.

Our worst times come when she refuses to nap. She's three and a half now, and many of her friends have given up their naps, but she still seems to need hers. (She sleeps like a rock once she's out, and behaves monstrously if she stays awake.) Still, I've been living for a year with the guilty sense that I'm *forcing* her to sleep, imposing naps on her tyrannically for my own convenience. Nearly half the time I have for my own writing comes during her naps, and the possibility that she'll deprive me of even one day's session drives me almost to hysteria. The day after she moved from a crib to a bed, she came out of her room nine times, frustrating me to the point of rage. I lost my patience, screamed at her, and finally pinned her down by her arms on the bed. "Don't *do* that, Daddy," she sobbed, and I saw myself in a stark light: selfish, violent, and wrong. It was the low point of my life as a parent.

Remorseful, I gave her everything she asked for (TV, ice cream, candy), and recognized in that overcompensation a second defeat.

Most days, though, she sleeps well in the afternoon, and we enjoy each other's company for the hour before supper. Sometimes we play baseball in the unfinished basement (last month she managed to hit the red ball with the big purple bat for the first time), or get fries at Burger King and share them while doing the grocery shopping, or blow bubbles in the backyard with the neighbor's granddaughters. When we're having fun together—energetic fun, the kind that requires me to gear up and overcome my middle-aged inertia—I enjoy myself more than I have in years. She asks for ballet music; I put *The Nutcracker* on the turntable, and we dance together like Baryshnikov and Thumbelina. I twirl her overhead (watch out for that ceiling fan!) and leap ridiculously across the living room, and she laughs a laugh of total satisfaction. She wants this dance to never end.

Jennifer and I take turns making large pots of food on the weekends, and we microwave the leftovers during the week. Dinner always begins as an enthusiastic mother-daughter reunion but often degenerates into a struggle to get Helen to eat. She would devour a ten-course meal if we let her eat in front of the television (I know because we used to do it), but at the table she nibbles just enough to take the edge off her hunger, and spends the rest of the time clowning. "Look at me!" she says, wearing a strand of spaghetti across her lip as a mustache. Jennifer loses her patience first, because this is the beginning of *her* time with Helen and she wants felicity, not a fight with a daughter who climbs down from her chair after three bites, saying, "All done."

If Jennifer's coaxing escalates to angry scolding, I sometimes intervene to avert war. Without planning or intending it, we fall into the roles of Good Cop and Bad Cop. It's not hard to see why: When one of us gets furious, the other one reflexively steps in to protect and reassure Helen. The amazing thing is how well it works—just like on TV.

(On the other hand, Helen's tantrums sometimes set off family battles. My wife has a temper of her own, and Helen's rages upset her even more than they do me. If she suppresses her anger at Helen, then it seethes inside her until she explodes at me instead. There is always some way in which the tantrum was my fault: I didn't give Helen enough notice before shutting the TV, I tried to fit too many activities into one day. To be criticized when my nerves are already on edge is intolerable, and so I shout louder than either of them, furious that I have to deal with two raging females instead of one. These are virtually the only fights Jennifer and I have, but it depresses me that we have them at all.)

After supper comes the handoff. While I clear the table in comfortable solitude, Jennifer takes Helen up to play in her room or take a bath. My wife would prefer that the three of us spend this playtime together, and I agree that it sounds idyllic, but the truth is, I stay away as long as possible. By the end of supper I've spent seven hours with Helen (more on weekends), and I don't think it's ogreish of me to want this time off.

The last hour or so before bed is Helen's sweetest time. We take turns reading to her while she eats her last snacks of the day, and she takes cuddling pleasure in the books, commenting enthusiastically and noticing connections between stories. ("Notre Dame Cathedral!" she cried when it appeared as a backdrop in *Madeline,* after she had watched her *Hunchback of Notre Dame* video several dozen times.)

The night rarely ends in complete harmony, though. "Good night, Helen," we say. "Sweet dreams. See you in the morning. *And don't come out.*" Futile words, because she always comes out of her room, as many as five times in a night. (I know, I know: This is the price of having her nap.) Jennifer and I huddle in my office because we don't want to go downstairs only to have to come back up five minutes later, when Helen emerges and says, "Something is wrong."

Except for sleep, dessert in the dining room is the only chance Jennifer and I get to be alone together. By this time, though, both of us are usually too tired to talk much. We resolve to get baby-sitters and go out more often, but the resolution never lasts more than a month or two. We're falling into a deadly pattern; we see ourselves falling, but we're too exhausted to catch ourselves. I keep hoping we'll do better in the future.

What a distance there is between my long-ago fantasies of fatherhood and the tired, irritable reality. I once saw a man in Riverside Park carrying his little son on his shoulders, and both of them were so radiantly happy that I grieved because I doubted I would ever find a wife, much less father a child. Back in my studio apartment I strummed my guitar and sang the Beatles' lullaby "Good Night" in a thin, high voice, sorrowing over the love I would never have a chance to give to a child of my own.

Since then, I've carried Helen on my shoulders dozens of times, just as blissfully as that stranger in the park—but now I know that there's much more to the story than ecstasy. When Helen comes out of her room after bedtime, I carry her back and sing "Good Night" to her with her head on my shoulder—but instead of heart-wrenching tenderness, what rises in me is impatience because she starts singing along with me and laughing, she won't go back to sleep, and I can't have even a half-hour alone with my wife.

*   *   *

Having described my days with Helen, I ask you: Would the account be any different if I were Helen's mother?

Or, to put it another way, are there differences between a father at home and a mother at home? I can only speak for myself because I've yet to meet another man who stayed home with his child. (To be honest, I've avoided meeting them, for fear they might turn out to be better fathers than I am, or else suicidally depressed.) The only real male/female differ-ence I've noticed is that I sneak more peeks at the newspaper than any mother I know, including at breakfast and lunch, when a better person would be talking to his daughter. Nevertheless, the stereotypical images of bumbling, irresponsible fathers—who let their children eat pink and purple junk food when Mom's not around, or who keep watching the ball game while the kids are climbing on the stove and exploring the knobs, or who can't say no when their little angels beg for hideous plastic monsters—all seem ludicrously unreal to me. They are stock characters from the sitcom division of America's collective unconscious; if they have any basis in reality, their models must be men who spend no more than an hour a week alone with their kids.

An astute observer could probably detect other differences between me and my female counterparts, but those differences would be dwarfed by what we share. Once you take on this job, it reshapes you. Your con-cerns become not those of a man or woman but of a Parent: finding activ-ities for your child that engage the body, mind, and spirit (and that get you through the day); creating a balance between rambunctious freedom and civility; locating toilets at the necessary intervals; and avoiding tantrums whenever possible. Every new mother must learn to be more patient and generous than she has ever been before; and fathers (if they choose the role instead of having it chosen for them by a layoff) are capa-ble of the same growth.

* * *

One thing I never expected to achieve is contentment. Yet for most minutes of most days, I find that I don't yearn for my life to change.

I may not be famous. I may not have won the National Book Award. But for the first time in my life, the disappointments don't outweigh the pleasures, and my daughter is the reason. Loving her and feeling connected to her has given me an alternate happiness; her affection counterbalances rejection. After twenty years of striving, I now have something to satisfy me, something more than hungry ambition. It seems I may even be able to enjoy my life.

At no time, not even during her tantrums, do I wish I had arranged things differently. Helen has become my joy, my most important responsibility, my identity. When we're apart for more than a few hours, I miss her intensely. (On a four-day vacation, while Jennifer's parents stayed with Helen, I took out my pictures at least three times a day to see her face.)

Having been home with her since she was three months old, I've had the extraordinary experience of watching her grow in tiny increments. Each day I've heard her say something she couldn't have said the day before. A few weeks ago this child who still says "fidgilator" (meaning that large appliance in the kitchen) expressed in metaphor the dread shared by all of the stay-at-home parents I know: holding a toy dinosaur's mouth up to my thigh, she said, "This dinosaur, he's going to eat the whole you, and there won't be any you anymore." But then she generously reconsidered and said, "Now he spit you out, and there's you again."

I'm so proud of her—proud when strangers call her adorable, proud when her teachers marvel at her politeness (instead of saying, "More juice!" like the other kids, she says, "Could I have a refill?"), proud that she has the desire and ability to make people laugh. Though they might find it odd if they knew that my wife is the one who supports our family, strangers on the street glow at the sight of a father and daughter who enjoy each other so much. As much as any mother, I derive a sense of justification from Helen. No longer do I steel myself for gatherings of family or friends because I still haven't reached my goal; now I take pride in being the father of a spunky girl whose antics draw smiles wherever we go.

Staying home with Helen has strengthened me and relaxed me. When we're together, I walk with a calm confidence that I never felt before. I no longer worry whether anyone—neighbor, friend, or relative—thinks I'm a failure or a success.

*   *   *

I've achieved a certain comfort, in both my household and my town. I've met parents and children through Helen's nursery school and have turned playground encounters into friendships. But my comfort is about to be exploded.

In less than a month our second child will be born, and I'm terrified. I dread the further narrowing-down of my worktime, I fear Helen's jealousy, and I don't know how I will get through another year of caring for an infant. (Starting from scratch again when it took so long to get this far!) True, it won't be as lonely with Helen there to keep me company, but I'm almost four years older now, and the mere idea of a newborn makes me want to cover my head with a pillow again. I learned to be a father to Helen, but I haven't become so paternal that I'm happy to give up another chunk of my life to my children.

Tucked away among my complaints, though, one small consolation glimmers: Helen, who never stops changing, has grown more independent lately. She doesn't snuggle against me as much as she used to, and I miss our closeness. I'm thinking that it won't be so bad to have that warm, fleshy bond again with a second child, for a few years at least. It may not cancel out the frustrations that lie ahead, but there is sweet pleasure in the thought of another little person running into my arms and shouting, "Daddy!"

Turf Wars

MAXINE CHERNOFF

My twin sons were ready for kindergarten, but I wasn't prepared for the changes it would bring. For the first time they would be apart, having spent their preschool lives together at a sunny establishment run by a tribe of underemployed blond women. Their leader, Chuck, was an ex-hippie, who still wore suede headbands and fringed vests. A Caring World was landscaped with sunflowers, broken tricycles, and banners that proclaimed kindness to all. "Sharing Is Caring," "Enjoy Your Lunch!" "Be Kind to Each Other!" read the signs posted on the yellow cinder-block walls of the compound. Lunch was served family-style, the bathroom was of the unisex variety, and each winter a nonsectarian Christmas pageant precluded the issue of competition by allowing each and every child to dress as Santa. I had always wanted to see the room where thirty or more cottony beards were kept on special display the rest of the year.

Now A Caring World was becoming part of my sons' past while the present filled me with the exclusive dread that only mothers of twins can feel. It was the same dread I had first perceived when the ultrasound technician asked me if I had been noticing an unusual amount of activity in my womb. She had gone on to show me the two heads, four arms, and four tiny legs of the two children I had found myself miraculously carrying. How could this be, I asked myself with some discomfort, for if having another child was something I had desired, something that would enrich me and round out the meaning of my life, wouldn't having twins enrich me doubly so? "See their little turtles!" the technician continued, telling me in her odd variant of baby talk that she had located the sexual organs that further described my twins as boys.

My reaction had been similar to their future sister's response. At age nine she was a frank girl who already knew her mind. "Twin boys?" she wailed—and here I don't exaggerate. "I wanted one sister and I'm getting two brothers?" The brother part didn't concern me. I had always loved baseball and Westerns and other gender-inappropriate entertainments—even boxing and rodeos. Having sons to share these interests would give me back the feeling of having a father, a father who had died too young at age fifty-nine, twelve days after my wedding. But two? Twins brought out immediate worries about my health, my pregnancy, my ability to continue to teach, my prospects of ever sleeping again, writing again, or spending a moment of relaxed family time with my husband and daughter.

I managed to keep them inside me until my eighth month when both water bags suddenly broke (Yes! It's possible to have two amniotic sacs with fraternal twins.) We sped down Lake Shore Drive to the Women's Hospital, where a cesarean section was performed. Within five minutes of each other, out came two sons. Julian and Philip were healthy and beautiful and peaceful when they eventually slept (never at the same hours or through the same night). They began walking at nine months, within two days of each other, and their activity never stopped. I would scoop up one, then run to rescue the other from a pending crisis. A hundred books would begin to topple from a shelf one had swiped at like an angry woman breaking china. The cat would sit, straining to remain level-headed, as she waited for me to remove her tail from a mouth newly sprouting teeth. The radio would suddenly blare as one boy turned the dials from disco to swing to salsa while the other stomped and jumped in frantic circles.

One morning before I was able to rejoin them in the front room with a cut-up banana for a snack, they maneuvered the television off its base. The pop and fizzle of the screen as it fell on its face echoed in my ears for weeks.

The boys were normal and smart and sweet and impossible as most toddlers are, but life with twins was an assault on any preconceived notion of time and crisis management. It was preschool that had set our lives on track again. Every day I had four hours to regain my composure, reorganize blasted zones of the house, make a pot of coffee, and, yes, even write a story now and then. Their hours away from home had convinced me that a rewarding life after twins was indeed a possibility. My husband, daughter, and I could have gotten monogrammed shirts saying "Twin Survivor," but we mostly missed them in the house and spent many hours of their absence recounting their feats and triumphs.

Now it was time for another passage that would add further details to our saga of twin-rearing. The inseparable pair was about to walk into public school and go their own ways for the first time in their lives.

Maybe we shouldn't separate them, I argued to myself, but I also considered the problems that staying together posed for the more cooperative, less assertive twin. Just as the family had endured twins, Philip had suffered years of Julian's fussy dominance and deserved a break. Philip had been held by strangers on airplanes when colicky Julian demanded my attention. He had surrendered the best toys to his brother. A photo of both boys in the bathtub catches Julian in the act of plundering a washcloth that Philip had been happily sucking. Despite this abuse, Philip had spoken Julian's name before that of his older sister or his father or myself. He had developed kindness and patience beyond his years at the hands of his brother, but there were costs. If the twins weren't separated, I imagined how Philip would continue to hold back.

Signs of this syndrome had already emerged. Despite Philip's warmth, verbal precocity and general charm at home, I had already received disturbing phone calls from preschool attendants at A Caring World: "Philip doesn't know his name." "Philip doesn't know how to color." "Philip isn't joining in games." These were acts of commerce and communication that Julian the Eager accomplished on both their behalfs. Philip clearly needed the chance to make his way that a separate kindergarten experience would provide.

With much difficulty in Chicago's socially engineered magnet school program, I found them a science and math academy that had room for two male Caucasians in two different classrooms at the kindergarten level. As mothers of twins know—for who expects ever to have twins—stories have their complications. Once again Fate played its fickle hand when Julian was given the beloved veteran teacher who made origami swans and played the recorder in a brightly lit, gaudily decorated classroom that resembled kindergarten heaven. Philip received a middle-aged, insecure rookie who looked too large for her environment of small chairs, miniature scissors, and downsized brooms, rakes, and plastic produce.

This circumstance is a perfect symbol of the dilemma of the mother of twins. All the inequities of life get summarized daily in their experience. "Life isn't fair!" is laid as a template over every situation. A minor version of *Sophie's [godawful] Choice* is enacted daily.

To my great relief, neither boy complained about his separation or his unequal learning experience. Although Philip's average teacher paled next to Julian's exceptional one, both boys made good progress and seemed happily settled—until recess reared its ugly head.

The problem with recess was Philip's loyalty to his brother—loyalty transcending classroom and regional boundaries. It is hard to understand how thirty days in kindergarten can cause children to claim their turf and become as warlike as the tribes of naked boys in *Lord of the Flies,* but when Philip came over to visit his brother one morning, he was "attacked" by several other children who didn't want him in their territory. They punched him and knocked him over and told him to leave. That morning I received a call from school that Julian had been in a fight. The school was unable to provide further details.

When my boys got home that afternoon, I met them where the school bus dropped them off every day. Before they had reached the door to our house, they were already enthralled in their story. Julian had risen to the occasion by turning on his new classmates. He had pounded a child named Tolu (later to become one of his best friends) in defense of his brother's inalienable right to a visit.

It was clearly the moment to celebrate their victory, a victory that had gone unexplicated to teachers who knew little of the psychology of twins. Having become a twin expert by necessity, I would ultimately share my insights with teachers when other invisible or unexamined episodes of jealousy, anger, or collaboration got enacted on school grounds.

Meanwhile, I delighted in the details of the blows that Julian had landed out of justice and love. The narrative contained drama, conflict, hyperbole, and figurative language. Its teller was Philip, chronicler of Julian's triumph. I marveled at my sons' resilience and love as I listened to their modern mini-epic about the reunion of two brothers whose loyalty to each other was deeper than any devotion to their new tribes.

Atalanta:
The Riddle of Fathers and Daughters

GORDON CHURCHWELL

The moment I have been dreading for months.

Olivia, my two-year-old daughter, splashes across the tidal basin of our bathtub—littered with boats and wind-up sea life—and up the length of my body to arrive somewhere mid-thorax. She wants to play her favorite game of the moment, which I jokingly refer to as the Young Frankenstein Game: naming body parts. She starts with her favorites, the eye and the ear—favorites because she can actually semi-pronounce the names. The eye, of course, is all of one vowel, and as for the ear, well, let us just say the consonant is disposable. After dispensing with my head, she points to the two tan dots on my chest. I weigh my options, and I settle on the relatively fail-safe solution. "These are Daddy's 'nipples,' " I say, knowing that the "pl" combination is mostly beyond her powers of mimicry.

But tonight is different because up until now she has ignored the eight-hundred-pound gorilla of body parts (which in my case, I must admit, is merely an average-sized chimpanzee): my penis, of course, bobbing benignly in the bathwater like a miniature buoy. She swats at it and laughs.

"No, honey. You don't want to hurt Daddy, do you?"

"That'n?" she demands.

I pause for a moment, again weighing my options. What one is afraid of here is not the word *penis,* because, after all, words are at this point merely little signposts for her. They are unburdened with social significance. What one is afraid of is that these verbal signposts can readily stand in for many like things; that the word "apple" could also be applied to tomatoes, oranges, and boccie balls. And so what one is afraid of is her using her amazing verbal miming abilities to carry the word *penis* into the world with her indiscriminately. Especially the next time she is at playgroup and the mommies and nannies are serving the favorite food of all kiddies, hot dogs.

Luckily, there is a solution to almost every fear. "Weenie, honey. It's Daddy's weenie."

Then she points to her vagina. I have to think for a moment. I then remember a similar bathtub conversation my wife, Julie, had with her the other day.

"That's your 'weewee,' honey."

"Mom-Mom?" she asks.

"Mom-Mom has a weewee, too."

Satisfied, she splashes off without another thought. My own being— alas, I have been found out.

*　　*　　*

I first met Atalanta in my junior year of college. Her name was Kitty. She was the number one player on the woman's tennis team. She carried herself with more confidence than anyone I can remember from those years. Now that I think of it, I'm almost sure I was secretly in love with her.

Atalanta was the favorite Greek myth of my childhood. A little strange, isn't it? Why would a boy have the Atalanta myth as his favorite story?

Atalanta is a complex girl. Her father abandons her on a mountainside hours after her birth because he wants a son. She is rescued and suckled by a she-bear and later raised by hunters. She grows up into an athletic phenom, so skilled a hunter that she takes part in the boar hunt of Calydon—which was an all-male event until she showed up. Later, when she decides she is ready for marriage, she issues a challenge. She will marry any man who can beat her in a foot race. Finally, after a long unbeaten streak, Atalanta meets her match. A guy named Hippomenes beats her with the aid of the goddess Aphrodite, who gives him three golden apples taken from the garden of the Hesperides. As he begins to fall behind, Hippomenes throws the apples onto Atalanta's path. She stoops to pick them up, and in the delay, Hippomenes wins the race and wins Atalanta as his wife.

To a young boy, Atalanta's actions were a mystery. She could have won the race. What could those golden apples have represented? What value could possibly compare with her unbeatable status?

As I grew into young manhood, the fascination with Atalanta continued. Of course by this time I knew a few more things and so realized that Aphrodite lurking in the background was probably significant. From my standpoint, however, it still didn't make any sense for her to compromise her excellence. What need in Atalanta did those apples represent? It also bothered me that they were made of gold. I mean, the damned things didn't do anything. They didn't give her any powers, they didn't foretell the future. I rationalized: Maybe she wanted to get caught? Maybe she realized it was time to stop running her own race and join the human race? Anyway, it was a riddle.

I remember an adventure at the end of senior year. A group of us were going skydiving: five guys and Kitty. I was doing it partly because I had a wicked nihilistic streak but also because I had to make up several gym credits in order to graduate. I had struck a bargain with the devil in the form of the athletic director, who was a friend of mine. One jump certificate and a case of beer, and I was a free man. I said, What the hell. My life wasn't worth a damn in those days anyway.

Kitty, on the other hand, was in it purely for sport.

The lowly Cessna groaned like an overloaded pickup truck, straining to get up to three thousand feet. The five of us guys looked awful. I had drunk nearly a bottle of Scotch the night before in order to gather my courage. I suspect my compadres had done the same. At one point in the evening I can remember lying flat on my back on a campus path. My girlfriend had her ear to my chest listening for a heartbeat. The morning of the jump, I vomited, drank some coffee to calm my nerves, started in on a pack of Marlboros, and prepared to meet my maker.

Over the jump site, the jumpmaster motioned for us to get ready. We five amigos looked at each other with rodent-like fright in our eyes. Only Kitty moved confidently toward the open door. I still remember that moment, the wind clawing at her legs. Even with her jump helmet on, the ends of her hair floated weightless and free. She was magnificent.

She looked back at us and grinned. She gave us hapless five a thumbs-up and yelled, "Last one down is a rotten egg!" And then she was gone.

One thing about Kitty, she didn't need us.

Atalanta: The Riddle of Fathers and Daughters

* * *

Consider this. The Huaoroni of the Amazon tell a story about a dark period of their history.* According to legend, Huaoroni men had to deliver their babies via cesarean section because their wives had not learned the muscular action necessary to push the infant out of the womb. Thus the Huaoroni husbands lost their partners at birth and had to raise their children alone. Only when a wise forest rodent called a *wegonhue* taught one laboring woman the proper technique did the unfortunate cycle stop.

I don't know what this sounds like to you, but it sounds like leverage to me: Huaoroni men keeping their place in the story of reproduction and preserving their importance as fathers.

In contrast, two years into parenthood, I sometimes find myself the regretful owner of a penis. In our gender-obsessed and conflicted time it's just not the desired appliance for parenthood. It's like having a loaded gun in the house—or a sign that flashes "Kick Me!"

If I sound a little testy, I think it's important to consider for a moment the contradictions that men live with as fathers and how our society's peculiar brand of fin-de-siècle flux intrudes on the personal life of parents.

First, the lack of cultural guidance. Cultures—in the form of traditions and other indigenous narratives—use stories to pass down roles and guide behavior in ways that are tacit yet fundamental. From these stories descend the meanings we need to plod forward through the dull

* All references to the Huaoroni are drawn from *Androgynous Parents and Guest Children: The Huaorani Couvade* by Laura Rival of the University of Kent at Canterbury, published in the *Journal of the Royal Anthropological Institute*, December 1998.

tasks of the quotidian. What happens if those stories don't exist or are in the process of being altered and rewritten?

Certainly our culture is without a lot of positive stories about men *qua* men in general, and certainly few encouraging stories of men as fathers. Consider what the "experts" have to say. When we are emotional and loving toward our babies, it is described as "engrossment," a patronizing and pathologizing term invented by psychologists and other social scientists who, I might add, have been responsible for some of the more ridiculous ideas of the last 150 years. The other day I had to suffer through a *New York Times* article titled "Daddy Dearest: Do You Really Matter?" the gist of which is that little scientific research exists on fathers, and the little that does hasn't been able to establish just what it is we do that's important. All this proves, of course, is that the belief in science and scientists as the legitimizing authority for all reality is our culture's peculiar brand of insanity.

Add to this all of the other gender issues that float around in a marriage, and you end up with a situation where I often feel I have to earn trust every day. Without stories, without culturally defined roles acceptable to both partners, men constantly have to improvise, and while improvisation can be exciting, it isn't necessarily reliable. The simplest child care request or comment from Julie can set off a cascade of mind-digesting questions. What will it mean if I do this? Will she think I'm a good father? Should I have thought of it first? What will it mean if I refuse? How come I don't get to make my own parenting mistakes when she makes so many herself? How many diapers add up to enough diapers?

Is it any wonder that when Olivia was born, along with joy was delivered enormous anxiety? I felt apprehensive about what was to come because at the heart of most partnerships today is a paradox: How can a man who is making the transition to being a father possibly feel comfortable in a society that has overturned or discarded most of its definitions of fatherhood? Further, while all of this doubt is bad enough in a general sense, consider it in the specific: What possible contribution can a man feel he can make in bringing up a little being who will one day become a woman?

Since my own culture offers me little, every morning I awake to invent myself as a father. What makes it bearable is the knowledge that every morning Julie has to invent herself as a mother. Bonding may be instinctual, but parenting is not. All it takes is a visit to the monolithic Family Section of the nearest Barnes & Noble to realize that women know nothing and have to learn everything. All it takes is listening to my own mother give parenting advice to confirm this—and to make me wonder how I, along with countless generations, survived childhood.

This true state of things is a comfort to me.

While improvisation is unreliable, it is also exhilarating—like being at the door of an airplane, staring out at the earth below and the curvature of space. It's fun to think about how far ahead of our culture's curve we are as parents, and to think how far behind social trends are the social scientists.

The wise Huaoroni weigh in with an interesting perspective. To them having a child *creates* the actual marriage. Wife and husband are reborn as mother and father during the birth process. The rituals that both man and wife go through during the birth process are in essence a second marriage.

I feel that way. Being forced to make things up as we go along, to invent, to create, to cobble together, has also given us the chance to write the true story of our marriage. This, I think, was what Julie and I intended all along when we chose to be parents: to jump through the slick, ambivalent surface of contemporary life into meaningfulness; to live lives of gravity.

Almost every day of Olivia's life we've had something to put down into the legend: nursing Julie through the first weeks of postpartum depression. Taking turns through winter nights, a colicky baby strapped to one of our chests, plodding the miles to sleep. Holding each other for an hour and a half the first time we tried to "Ferber-ize" Olivia. Saving Olivia from choking on her first birthday—a malignant pellet of chicken bone popping into Julie's hand as I whacked Olivia on the back.

These stories are now the OED of our marriage and the beginning of a new identity for me. Satisfying as they are, there is still a secret desire that I harbor: to know distinctly my relationship with Olivia, to know what my contribution is to her—not as the slightly secondary half of a parental team, but as a father.

The answer, I think, lies in the profound difference in Olivia's emotional response to the two of us. With her mother she is ineffably bonded. In most instances, Julie's merely leaving the room elicits whimpers, then howls of protest, while her father—desperately trying to distract her by mimicking all known North American mammals, and so forth—barely gets noticed. Conversely, there are times when it is far easier for me to get Olivia to do things than it is for Julie. Olivia is often cooperative and compliant about having me change her diaper, put her to bed, get her dressed in the morning, and a whole host of other routines that, with Julie, often escalate into ponderous, near-operatic exchanges. These successes, however, often leave me feeling uneasy and ambivalent. Balanced against convenience is the suspicion that she cooperates because deep down, at some evolutionary level, she fears me.

Then there are those special moments that I truly call my own. I'm not quite sure how to characterize them, but if I had to guess, I would say that they have something to do with Olivia's comfort with risk-taking. Let me give you an example. At some point during a bath, when it's time to get down to business, like now, I call Olivia over and announce that I am going to wash her hair and face. She protests with the lamentations of a guillotine candidate—she hates water on her face—but eventually she sits down in my lap. I lather her head, rubbing away the remnants of her cradle cap, and rinse out the soap by carefully tilting her head back and running water through her hair. Then with a washcloth I wipe down her face and her rosebud lips, paying special attention to extract the hardened, day-old rubbish in her nose.

Not Julie. Not her baby-sitter. Me. I'm the only person on the planet who can perform this procedure without causing a major meltdown.

That is what I call trust.

*   *   *

Several years after I graduated, I met Kitty again. It was at an alumni function at my alma mater's New York club. I saw her across the room, standing in the middle of a circle of gray pin-striped flannel types. I knew disappointment awaited me, but I slowly worked my way across the room until I stood next to her. "Geronimo," I said.

She smiled and we talked. She worked for some bank, which I had already figured out from her clothing. She introduced me to a handsome but nondescript guy standing next to her, an ex-jock who worked on Wall Street. The whole thing was so boring that his name didn't stick. It bounced off my slackening face and slid to the carpet to lie among the fallen remains of peanuts and crudité. By way of consolation, I told my-self that this is what happens when you grow up. Everyone compromises, even Kitty. But inside I knew the truth. Our society's conventional ex-pectations had ruined her.

After the requisite pleasantries, I chose the earliest possible moment to leave. The circumstances were too confining for my memories. The gray flannel of her suit was so much ash on a dampened fire.

Alas, Kitty, what have you done? You always had a weakness for frat boys.

I think it was then that I understood the price of the golden apples.

* * *

Over the years I have become amazed at the power of stories to shape our behavior—but not for the reasons you might think.

Perhaps it was some old guy at the University of Chicago who said that symbols are ultimately irrational or at least supra-rational. They gather power because they are ultimately irreducible. They explain but cannot be explained.

I have come to understand this in my own life. The boy who was fas-cinated by the Atalanta myth in childhood went on to meet Atalanta throughout his life. He remained puzzled, and the mystery drove him on.

I can remember once in a campus bar being approached by a girl. She was in my American Intellectual History seminar. Earlier that day I had stood up in class and declaimed loudly and lengthily about some pet half-baked ideas of mine. Those ideas, I can assure you, were very forget-table; however, I do remember scoring some points with the professor.

Anyway, this girl is complimenting me on my performance in class. I remember being amazed. Why is this woman stooping to admire me? By all measurable standards I'm sure she is smarter. She also reads the material and comes prepared to class. With all of that diligence and talent why wasn't she the one making like Daniel Webster? In fact, why did all of the women in the class, whom I would describe as at least equally as gifted as the men and always better prepared, seem so reticent? With their potential to run, why did they choose to plod?

Perhaps I could have told her that it was the most natural thing in the world for me to take a chance, to intuit and even revel in the idea that success required multiple failure. That finding one redemptive idea often meant appearing radical, even foolish. That sometimes you have to throw words and ideas like dice to find out where you have to go. That the going there takes a lifetime and is lonely.

Of course, I couldn't tell her then what I only know now. Looking back, I believe it was during this evening that my unconscious made a pact with itself and shaped my future. Someday I would have a daughter, and I would teach her how to be strong, self-reliant, and outspoken.

I would also teach her how to gamble.

* * *

My greatest fear as I started out on this journey of parenthood was thinking that it would be me who would provide the golden apples, unconsciously slipping them into Olivia's mental lunchbox as she headed to school each day. This golden apple is the need for approval. This golden apple, the craving for validation. This golden apple, a reverence for consensus.

Once I attended a lecture at my wife's alma mater, a fancy Upper

East Side private girls' school. The guest speaker was Catherine Steiner Adair, a colleague of Carol Gilligan, the famous female developmental researcher. She explained how girls tend to do exceedingly well until the fourth grade. At this point they suddenly become less sure of themselves, have less ability to make simple and fundamental choices, are less confident about being the author of their own lives, and have their self-esteem tied up in who their friends are. This was the beginning of the "tyranny of kind and nice," as she described it, when girls are asked to put aside cruder feelings of anger and competitiveness for more socially acceptable displays of emotion. It is also at this point that they become vulnerable to Madison Avenue depictions of the ideal female form, worry about their weight, and start to suffer eating disorders.

Of course what was implicit in her talk is that our patriarchal society is at the root of all these problems. She noted in passing that 83 percent of girls in one study she had conducted perceived their fathers as "unable, unwilling, or uninterested in knowing who they are."

I remember thinking, while she implored the mothers in the crowd—most of whom appeared to be fashionably thin and dressed by Madison Avenue designers—to be better role models for their daughters, that women are confronted with a perverse paradox. Being a role model cuts two ways. Mothers can be pillars of empowerment, but they are also the most direct link between female compromise and male expectations. Perhaps it was the fathers in the audience who could contribute something of their very own to tip the balance.

It is a crude idea, but somehow it has merit. To compete and find your way as a girl and then a woman in a world where so many of the rules remain male perhaps requires the teachings of a father—especially a father for whom maleness and male rules hold no mystery, magic, or veneration.

What if Atalanta's father did not abandon her on the mountainside at birth but instead loved her and cherished her? What if it was he who raised her and not a she-bear or strangers, and taught her to stand her ground before the Calydonian boar's charge? Taught her to guide her spear into its heart with all the relentless courage and focus that our daughters should use to find the heart of all matters? Especially, the central, self-actuating myths that hold the truth of their lives.

And what if he explained the price of the golden apples so that she could choose without compromise?

As we leave the bath, Julie takes over. I can hear them in the other room as Julie gets her ready for an outing to a Japanese restaurant. Olivia whining and fussing. Julie negotiating. Olivia whining and fussing. And so on.

Both of us wish for Olivia a selfhood of her own choosing. It is our most cherished idea, the most important idea of our marriage. And over our two years of parenthood, I have been grateful that Julie has trusted me to be a parent on my own terms, with my own contributions.

What will be interesting to watch over time is what we each give toward that goal. While Olivia is more emotionally involved and attached to Julie, I often wonder whether it is help or hindrance. Between them there is a profound bonding that seems to know no boundaries—boundless in love as well as entanglement. From me Olivia seems to expect less and as a result looks more to herself. Ours is not as profound a relationship, but it is ultimately more free.

This is a comfort to me.

*   *   *

After dinner we step out onto the street and head home. Olivia takes off. Ever since she learned to walk, she has preferred to run. After a few calls of protest, we are quickly after her.

At the first cross street, there are no cars coming, so I let her cross, running. The blocks pass. Julie and I run ahead of her, scouting for cars. Sometimes I signal to make sure they stop. Sometimes I pick Olivia up and whisk her across and set her back down before she can protest.

She runs on. Past the Arab livery drivers who look up from their storefront card game and cheer her on. Past the Korean green market where a startled grocer moves his sidewalk cartons aside so she can pass. Past the ice-cream store where a group of teenage girls point and twitter in amazement. Past the many faceless passersby who turn and whisper, "Look at that little girl!" The little girl whose face is an expression of boundless, fearless joy.

By later calculation, she runs almost a half-mile before she trips on a crack in the sidewalk and falls onto her hands. She cries, as much out of exhaustion as pain. I comfort her, stroking the back of her head as she buries her face in my shoulder.

Someday when she is older, I will tell Olivia the story of Atalanta. I am already preparing it, testing out various story lines. I can tell you that in one version there will be no need to mention the golden apples.

In Love with Boys

ROSEMARY L. BRAY

*M*ornings are hard on night birds like me, and children are harder still. It is my destiny to be blessed with two small boys who delight in early rising, and delight even more in me. My name is the first word each utters in the morning, and often the last on their lips at night. My sons love their father; I know they do. They clutch at his leg, they wrestle him to the floor, they delight in his threats to recycle them as he carries them upside down through the house. But they are in love with me—and we all know it.

"Mommy!" My son Daniel, not quite two years old, is calling me from the crib in his guttural voice by 7 A.M. Not long after, his older brother Allen, already a model of sophistication at age five, has entered our room (without knocking) and climbed into our bed, wedging himself between my husband and me, and tucking his head just beneath mine. "Good morning, Mommy. I just want to lie down a little," he announces.

After a few restless minutes, I rise to get Daniel, who never ceases calling me until I appear at the door. Lately he has taken to screaming with pleasure at the sight of me, then jumping up and down in his crib, bouncing so high I fear he'll crack his head on the slanted ceiling. This morning is no different. He holds out his arms to me in a kind of ecstatic greeting, and as I reach down to pick him up, he wraps his arms around my head and presses his face to mine, as though he were trying to climb through to the other side of my head. "My mommy!" he says, and makes a big smacking kiss sound that he learned from me.

No one could have told me how delicious it is to have the unqualified adoration of small boys. My sons believe everything I tell them, are convinced there is nothing I cannot do, rest assured in my power to alter every aspect of their universe. I hate it that they'll learn that all I can really do is love them with all my heart. But I don't have to tell them that just yet. For now, I can bask in the glow of perfection they cast over me.

When I first learned I was pregnant, six years ago, I longed for a girl. My mother and I have always been close, and once I began thinking of a life with children, I envisioned a life of shared pleasures with a daughter. True, I had never been into baking and Barbie dolls, but neither were my mother and I, and we'd found plenty to talk and laugh about through the years. I expected the usual adolescent minefield—there were three years when I'm sure my mother wanted to give me away—but I figured my daughter would outgrow it just as I did. I looked into the future and saw a girl like the girl I had been, attached to and adoring the mother I hoped to become.

What a rude awakening I was destined to have! After learning that the genetic testing my doctor required revealed the presence of a healthy fetus, the nurse on the other end of the phone asked if I wanted to know the sex of the baby. Of course I wanted to know; why should strangers in Philadelphia know what I was having while my husband and I remained in the dark?

"Are you sure?" she asked. "Some folks want to be surprised."

I figured since no one really knows what their children are like till they get here, that would be surprise enough for me. "I really do want to know," I told her, keeping a grip on my patience.

"You're having a boy!" she announced with glee, and I felt my stomach drop. For some reason I just assumed God and the universe would look into my heart, know my secret desires, and present me with a girl. I was so sure, in fact, that I hadn't even thought seriously of boys' names.

I called my husband at work to tell him that the testing was done and the baby was fine. "Did they tell you what we were having?" he asked me.

"Yes, but you said you didn't want to know; you said it didn't make a difference to you."

"It doesn't make a difference," he told me. "But if you're going to know, I think I should know."

I was surprised that he couldn't tell from the hurt in my voice. "She said it's a boy."

"Yes!" Bob shouted into the phone.

"I thought you didn't care what we had," I said, stung by his happiness.

"I guess I cared more than I thought."

I know I cared. And I was afraid. Now my visions were of a lonely old age, abandoned in a nursing home while my wild son cavorted through life, waiting for me to die. Some part of me knew I wasn't being fair. But I didn't understand boys, I reasoned. What would I have to say to a boy? How could I keep him from growing up with a disrespect for women that was rampant in the culture? And we are an African-American family, which meant I had to ask myself: How well could I keep him alive in a culture that ignored black women and feared black men? A girl I could protect; a boy would cause me worry every day of my life.

As the months passed and my sorrow about my nonexistent daughter eased, so did my anxiety about the raising of this seemingly alien being. One friend who had preceded me into motherhood and was raising a boy and a girl put it succinctly: "The one thing nobody tells you—so I'm going to tell you—is that boys absolutely love their mothers. It's not that my daughter doesn't love me. But Damon loves the ground I walk on, and that's the truth."

I really didn't need such slavish devotion, I said to myself. All I want is a chance to be close to my children when they're grown. This fear of raising a stranger or a psychopath or someone destined to die young joined a list of several dozen other fears visited on other prospective parents that recede but never really disappear. I was, in short, driving myself crazy.

When Allen was born, I came to regard him with an attitude I can only describe as slavish detachment. I couldn't quite believe I was someone's mother, and so this little being born from me couldn't really be mine, I thought. Allen was preternaturally self-possessed as a baby and seemed to regard me, at first, with a similar lack of conviction. And yet neither of us could leave the other alone. I carried him from room to room, showered with the bassinet in the bathroom and the shower curtain wide open (it's a wonder he didn't drown), watched him sleep, and then woke him up in an attempt to ensure his continued ability to breathe. Seemingly indifferent to me even in play, he seemed most focused on me whenever I nursed him.

And then one day at 3 A.M., when he woke screaming to be fed and changed, I stumbled through my maternal duties and was preparing to put Allen back to bed when he looked at me and smiled. Nearly every mother is tortured in the early days of her child's life, deprived of sleep and bored by the endless repetition of thankless tasks. And just when you don't think you can take another moment, this child really sees you, really responds to you as mother for the first time, and if you weren't already in love, you are then. I was thoroughly in love.

But the bliss of cuddling an infant gave way all too soon to the uncertainly of raising a little boy, an uncertainty burdened with conflicting opinions about the mother's role in a boy's life. Already the mixed signals were there. Love him—but not too much. Pay attention to his emotional life—but don't make a baby of him. One book suggested a slow but steady withdrawal from my boy as he grew, the better to enable him to enter the world of men. Another suggested that I was simply not able to help him become a man, so I should turn him over to his father.

Thankfully, Allen never read any of my contradictory texts. He continued to climb up on the couch to sit between Bob and me, turning toward each of us in turn with joy, calling us MamaDaddy. To him we were—and are—an inseparable unit. In a way I had never fully appreciated before, I grew more grateful than ever for my happy marriage. The contentment Bob and I had found with each other mattered not just to us but to this boy who, along with his little brother, would grow up with the image of a loving partnership between a black man and a black woman. It shouldn't matter to me quite so much, but it does.

It matters just as much to know that, for all the boy behavior that startled me (including Allen's biting of his toast into the shape of a gun and his accidentally running headlong into doors without uttering a whimper), I am the mother of two creatures supposed not to exist: sweet and sensitive African-American boys. Daniel may fight with two-year-old abandon over a toy car, but if his opponent should cry, he is the kind of child who will stop to give the other boy a hug. Allen may tease me in vain to buy him a toy gun, but when he glimpses a news report about hurt and starving people, he asks me why God doesn't do something to help.

Neither Allen nor Daniel has yet been corrupted by the mythology of the wild and rageful black savage. They do not yet represent anger, power, raw sexuality, threat, danger, or evil. They are not yet an excuse for white flight, white backlash, or white liberal angst. For now they are just my babies, and I am just their mom. They go to school and play with lots of different children of different races and religions. They fight and make up with their many friends. They tease and console each other as brothers are wont to do. And for now they do it all without the burden of most of the permanent stereotypes of either blackness or maleness. I wish it could stay this way forever.

But nothing does, and already I can see creeping into their consciousness (and my own) the first threads of the racial/gender status quo. Leaning into the doorway of our minivan, I checked Allen for his lunch and his backpack, then moved to kiss him good-bye—and for the first time saw him flinch. "Someone might see me, Mom," he whispered. On the first morning of the new order, I was too stunned to do anything but back away and reenter the car with tears in my eyes. But by the next day I had recovered, and when I moved toward him again and watched him retreat, I reached out and held him firmly.

"You might as well know now," I told him. "Mothers kiss. I'll be kissing you good-bye for as long as I live, so you had better get used to it." He looked at me with wide eyes and a small smile as I kissed his cheek. "See you later, Mom," he said and ran into the gate, while Daniel babbled happily that it was "my turn" to go to school. It was the first skirmish in what I know is a war. I realized it probably assumed more importance than necessary, that I was too sensitive about something really minor and wholly developmental, such as a shunned kiss.

But I didn't care. I love my sons too much to give them up to the image of manhood thrust upon them, an image that will become even more twisted as they grow older and race inevitably comes into play. Long ago when I agonized over not being the home-all-day, pie-baking, endlessly patient mother that my own mother is, I decided that all I had to give my boys was myself; only being real with them would make up for all the other things I thought I ought to be but would never be.

Finally, quietly, I put away my childish wish for someone just like me. I have instead two someones who can be like me or unlike me as they choose. Mostly I have accepted my fears as a mother's lot, and I have chosen instead to revel in what it is I do have—the sweet unconditional love of people who think slime is wonderful and Power Rangers are cool, and who may be forever unable to distinguish the toilet bowl from the floor just beneath it. If I could just get them to sleep until 8 A.M., life would be perfect.

Wrestling with the Angel

YONA ZELDIS MCDONOUGH

All of my life I have been a passive Jew. Although born to Jewish parents, I was raised in an assimilated, secular household. We observed no holidays, participated in no rituals. Hanukkah—which we celebrated only once or twice during my childhood—was a tepid, lackluster affair hurriedly prompted, no doubt, by my vigorous campaigning for a Christmas tree. The only seders we ever attended were those hosted by some dear friends of my parents in a nearby city. Neither my brother nor I went to Hebrew school; my brother did not even have a bar mitzvah.

My parents, particularly my father, had their own spin on being Jewish. He was an ardent Zionist who had dropped out of college at twenty—the year was 1948—to emigrate to Israel. My mother, sixteen, followed him, and there they lived, amid "sand, shit, and flies," as my paternal grandmother described it, first in a kibbutz and later a moshev, for the next nine years. My older brother and I were born there, and although he has memories of his life in the desert, I was less than a year old when my family returned to the United States for good. Israel, and the resounding mythology of Zionism, was an important part of my upbringing, but as myth, it was all very abstract to a little girl growing up on Ocean Parkway in Brooklyn and wondering why she was the only Jewish girl in the class whose parents wouldn't join the local Jewish center. "Too bourgeois," said my quasi-Socialist father. For him the memory of Israel was reality enough to give shape and form to his spiritual yearnings. I, however, was clueless. I wanted only to belong and yet knew that I did not. I yearned not for religion per se, because I did not know what that was. Instead, I yearned for a sense of identity, a sense of my place in the vast and unfathomable scheme of things.

As I grew, my worries subsided, replaced by other, more compelling ones: boys, sex, love. My parents divorced, with much venom and bitterness, during my senior year in high school, and I spent the next several years trying to pick up the pieces left in the wake of their breakup.

When I married, at twenty-seven, it was to a man who was not of my faith. I was not at all troubled by this; in fact, I tended to imbue his New England upbringing—Victorian white clapboard house, backyard filled with lilacs, learning to skate on the local pond in winter—with a kind of bleary, Norman Rockwell sentimentality. I hadn't an inkling that the passive, familiar-as-an-old-shoe Judaism I had lived with for so long was soon to be tested beyond any expectation or prior experience. And the crucible in which that test took place turned out to be the children— first a son, then a daughter—that we had together.

James Redden McDonough was born in the spring of 1991. Since I had undergone amniocentesis and knew I was carrying a boy, I had just assumed we would have him circumcised. After all, I was a Jew, and this was what Jews did. But my husband, as lapsed and passive a Catholic as I was a Jew, wasn't so sure. Although he himself was circumcised, he had read enough recent literature on the subject to make him question the necessity of the procedure. We debated it hotly and in anguish for the three days I was hospitalized. The wonderful doctor who delivered our baby told us she could circumcise him, too—as long as he was in the hospital. Once we took him home, we were on our own. My husband did not want to be forced into making the decision simply based on the timing, so we didn't. James left the hospital intact.

Before, circumcision had always seemed a fine, if remote, practice connected more to matters of personal hygiene than to the distant covenant Abraham had made with God. But holding my days-old infant in my arms, I realized that there was nothing passive or remote about having one's own child circumcised. One had to take the knife and cut—if not literally, then by asking another to do it.

Finally, we did decide to circumcise him, because we were told it was medically preferable, because we thought he should look like his father, because he was a Jew. To have opted against it would have felt to me like a renunciation of my faith, which, for all my discomforts with it, I was unable at that point to make.

We received the name of an Orthodox obstetrician who was also a moyle and called him to arrange the event. Not having any experience with attending or planning a bris, I turned to my eighty-two-year-old grandmother for guidance. She told me to buy sweets and wine and "wear a nice dress." Since ours is a small, truncated family, I invited only a handful of people—my mother and her boyfriend, my grandmother, and the moyle. I bought an expensive, pale butter cream cake and a bottle of champagne. I dressed and waited for the moyle. He had instructed me not to nurse the baby less than thirty minutes prior to his arrival since the intense crying that was sure to follow would most likely cause him to vomit. But the moyle was late and the baby was wailing, so I nursed him anyway just to calm us both.

When the moyle finally arrived, he told me to either watch the procedure or leave the building. "He'll cry so loudly that if you hear but don't see him, you'll be convinced that he's dying. Either watch, so you can see that he's not, or leave." I left. But my husband stayed because he was one of the ones to hold James down.

I waited downstairs in front of my apartment building, staring at the pizza place across Second Avenue and sweating wildly with the heat and the anxiety. When I returned to our apartment, the deed was done. My husband's face was white and drawn; the baby's was red from screaming. The moyle hurried off, declining my offer of cake and champagne—as did my husband, who was too shaken to eat or celebrate; he downed a double scotch and left for a walk. I sat on the couch trying to nurse James, who twisted his tiny face away from the breast, not ready to be soothed but needing, no doubt, to vent his infant sense of rage and betrayal. My mother and her boyfriend wrung their hands, distressed at our distress; only my serene little grandmother lifted her glass in praise of all that had transpired.

Not long after this I asked my husband if he wanted to have our child baptized. Since he had been so accommodating on the issue of circumcision, I felt that I ought to at least pose the question. But I also said that if we were to do this, he would have to be the one to find the priest and make all the necessary arrangements. I somehow couldn't imagine myself having a conversation with a clergyman who would ask, "Are you a Catholic? No? Do you plan to raise the child as a Catholic? Well then, why are you here?" Good question. So I left it up to my husband, who considered it but then ended up doing nothing. I was at the time relieved, and then was ashamed of my relief. If you can't give him religion, I scolded myself, why should you feel relieved that your husband can't either? But although from a rather religious Catholic family—parochial school, a sister who was a nun—he shared my sense of alienation from traditional forms of observance. This, paradoxically enough, was one of the things that united us.

Now, years after the fact, my husband does not resent the circumcison, but we both feel angry that he played such an intimate role in it, especially when we learned that parents are never the ones to hold the infant during the ceremony. Why hadn't the moyle told us that? Why were we left in the dark?

That fact has colored and helped shape my own complicated relationship to the religious identities of my children. Where I looked for instruction and initiation, I found none. Where I hoped for meaning, there was none either. I wanted that bris for myself as much as for my son. I thought it would be a magic key to unlock a door that had been closed to me for so long. Have the bris and walk over the threshold. Feel, finally and at long last, that you understand, that you belong. But the door remained shut.

In the fall of 1995 we had a daughter, a *shane maidele* (pretty girl, in Yiddish) with blue eyes and the unlikely name of Katherine Constance McDonough. "Who's Katherine?" my still-feisty grandmother wanted to know, hoping I would relent and name the child for a dead relative in accordance with Jewish custom. "It's the name I always wished I'd had" was my honest reply. Thank God I didn't have to worry about circumcision this time around.

It is a matter of some interest (though no real comfort) to me that James and Kate will not be as alone in their amalgamated religious identities as they would have been one or two generations ago. Many of the children of our acquaintance are also from mixed marriages. Those families face their own similar sets of dilemmas. Some opt for one religion over the other; others try to do both; and many, like us, do nothing other than the most secular kinds of celebrations.

At Christmas we have a tree and presents because I can remember only too vividly the intense longing I had for such rites. I have explained to my son about Jesus but am careful to say that his role as redeemer and savior is something other people—Christians, like his father—believe in, but I do not. I have never told them the story of Santa Claus because I just can't seem to do it with any sincerity. And I dislike the idea of building an elaborate structure that I will only have to dismantle later on. I do mention the idea of winter solstice and have talked about how all the lights and decorations see us through the dark days of winter. So far, the glittering tree and its heaped offering of gifts have satisfied him. But I am all too aware that this won't always be so.

On Easter morning we have an egg hunt. The eggs are plastic or papier-mâché, and they open. Inside I have placed coins and, in some cases, small bills. I give my children each a basket to collect the eggs; they run madly around the house, hectic and feverish in their delight. I offer no explanation about the meaning of this event other than that the eggs—and bunnies, chicks, and lambs with which they are decorated—symbolize springtime and the earth's triumphant renewal of itself. So far these two events have constituted the sum total of the religious education they have received from us.

My mother, who feels profoundly guilty over her failure to create a coherent sense of religious tradition for her own children, has tried to rectify that with her grandchildren. At Hanukkah she appeared at our door with a beautiful antique brass menorah and a box of candles; though she didn't intone the prayers, she let my son light the candles while the baby pointed and gestured eagerly toward the flame. She and her boyfriend have even begun hosting seders in her apartment. Though extremely abbreviated, they do recount the story of the exodus from slavery to freedom; the seder plate is filled with the requisite symbolic foods. This past year my son read the four questions and later asked some more of his own. I let my mother's boyfriend—clearly enjoying his role as teacher and guide—answer them. As I watched all this, I had mixed feelings about her latter-day return to conventional ritual observance. Although I can understand why she is doing it now, I still feel (childishly, I know) obscurely angry with her for not doing this sooner, when it would have meant so much to me. Nor is the irony lost on me that I am in a sense following in her footsteps by not providing my own children with a sense of their Jewish heritage. And yet this heritage meant enough to her to spend nine years in Israel; it has never exerted as profound a claim on me.

My own private doubts and struggles with Judaism—its sanctimonious exclusivity, its relentlessly patriarchal values—would still exist even if I were married to another Jew. But they are exacerbated by the fact that the man to whom I am married is a Christian. As tenuous as my own connection to Judaism was as a child, I at least knew that my parents were both Jews and that on the level of pure identification I, too, was a Jew. My children have no such certainty.

My son, a Jew by birth and by rite, has little or no sense of what that means, although I see him bravely trying to puzzle it out. He asks me, while splashing in a tub filled with bubbles and boats, if he's Jewish. "Half Jewish," I explain, feeling foolish and insincere as I do it. "Mom is Jewish. Dad is Catholic. You're half and half." He says nothing at the time but days later tells me about how a boy in his kindergarten class came to school with a small Torah, which he showed to James. "You can only read this if you're Jewish," he said. James paused and replied, "Well, I can read half of it since I'm half Jewish." But in my heart I know there is no such thing as the half and half I feebly offered to him. God, if he exists, demands nothing less than the whole.

On another occasion, some months later, my son announces, "I'm not Jewish. Dad's not Jewish. Kate's not Jewish either. You're the only one who's Jewish in this family." When I remind him that in fact he is at least part Jewish, he says, "Come on. Do I look Jewish?" Clearly he's trying to make sense of it all, trying to find the meaning. Why can't I help him? Why, when I look down, are my hands empty? This seems to me like the small, unconquerable nugget that lies at the bottom of the subject, like the stone in the shoe, the pit in the fruit, the one that you can't swallow, dissolve, or imagine away no matter how hard you try.

Part of what inhibits me from talking to my children about religion is God—that is to say, I don't know how to explain something whose existence I am not entirely certain of myself. I have even avoided Bible stories—despite my fascination with their austere and stark presentation of events both secular and divine—for they are, finally, so centered on God, and my own confusion and ambivalence on this subject seem too daunting to explain, at least just yet. Perhaps when my children are older and can better understand ambiguity, I will tell them that I want, and at times even yearn, to believe in God; that I envy those for whom faith is a given, who accept the joys and miracles and also the cruelties and sorrows of life as a part of a larger unseen design whose pattern is too magnificent and terrible for the human mind to understand or know. Envy them, yes, but I cannot count myself within their number.

I have not been able to answer these questions in the seven years since my son was born. But as my daughter grows and adds her voice to the chorus, I feel an even greater urgency to somehow, in some way, be able to do so. If I can't, I will be tormented by my own negligence—for negligence it truly is, though not because I don't care or I don't try. It's just that most of my trying takes place in the private arenas of the heart and mind, wrestling with the peculiar angel that is mine. If religion is the map that guides us through the mysterious and fearful terrain of the soul, then I must give my children something concrete for their journey—a scrap, a hint—that they can take on their way. I haven't done too well thus far, but neither have I given up the struggle.

The Problem at the Center of the Universe

RICHARD PANEK

"*I* can't believe I'm seven already," my son says. "I'll be *eight* this year." A pause. "I can't believe I got so old so *fast*."

He can't believe it? I say nothing, though, because what can I say? He had been dressing for school, pulling on a shirt, when he drifted somewhere, mid-button, as if he were still inside a dream. I knew the look, and I knew to wait. One day he emerged from one of these reveries and, regarding a recent tragedy in the news, said, "That Kennedy family. They're just fading away like the morning dew." Today, it turns out he's been contemplating a not entirely unrelated topic, and one of his favorites: time, and the relentless passing thereof.

It's one of his younger brother's recurring themes, too. It's one of everybody's, I suppose, but when my three-year-old emerges from a minor daydream of his own a day or so later, what he announces is this: "I big. I *big* now."

In a way, such a vivid contrast between two children who have grown up in identical circumstances might seem persuasive evidence of the primacy of nature over nurture. Indeed, how each of these two boys has come to regard the passage of time—one son looking longingly to the past, the other optimistically to the future—does bear an unmistakable resemblance to who he was right from the start. My older son waited several days before opening his eyes for the first time, only to immediately squeeze them shut again for several more days, as if not yet willing to surrender the solitary darkness of the womb. My younger son, however, popped out wide-eyed even though he was several weeks premature. I carried him across the delivery room, searching his face, and was shocked to find him searching mine right back, nearly stopping me in my tracks with his borderline impertinence: *Okay, now what?*

The answer to that question, as it happens, is everything past the grasp of genetics, everything beyond the determinism of the double helix, everything, in other words, that falls on the nurture side of the equation. Yes, who my children are today is who they were at birth— only much, *much* more so. And as different as their inherent characters might be, what is just as revealing, I suspect, is how extreme their defining characteristics have become—the ways each boy has remained *so much* the same.

Blame it on birth order. Among the many Mysteries of Parenthood—those secrets that, as we members delight in informing nonmembers, you just can't fully appreciate until you're one of us—birth order may be the most accessible to outsiders, the one that you don't really need to be a parent to understand. Even *I* understood the importance of birth order, and when I became I parent, at the age of thirty-two, I knew nothing about children. Once, I was talking to my older sister on the phone while she simultaneously carried on a conversation with her daughter in the background, and I remember thinking about my niece, who was maybe two at the time, "What's *wrong* with her? Can't she see her mother's on the *phone*?" As I say: *Nothing.* Yet when my older sister had her second child, even I knew enough to joke that the firstborn was sure to be jealous. How did I know? For the same reason I also knew to re-mind my sister that when I was a baby she used to hold me by the arms and swing me around the room until I cried, and to ask her, meanly, if she planned on subjecting her own kids to that kind of treatment. "Oh, *no*," she gasped, seeing my meanness and raising it. "I *love* my children."

What's remarkable here is not that my older sister tormented me but that I knew she had—that I knew the details of how she'd gotten away with it (waited until our parents were out of the room), how I responded (cried and cried and cried), how she responded when our parents came running back into the room to see what the hell was going on (blank look, shrug). All this had taken place at an age when I wouldn't possibly be able to remember it, yet apparently my older sister had made sure to tell me about it at an age when I *would*.

Such cruelty makes perfect sense. After all, to the firstborn falls the burden of believing he's the center of the universe at least until some-thing comes along to dethrone him—and often that something is a sib-ling. The rage at this displacement from his rightful position into a peripheral orbit, and especially at the bearer of these unfortunate tidings, should come as no surprise. Just look what they did to Galileo.

But by the time I was ready (I use the term loosely) to become a par-ent myself, my understanding of the potential impact of birth order was beginning to expand beyond the simple indignities one sibling might visit on another. Shortly after our first son was born, a friend with a couple of kids of his own recalled some old saying about how parents bathe the first child every day, bathe the second child once a week, and send the third child outside when it rains. It wasn't particularly funny then either, but it did make a point I hadn't previously considered: Like it or not, my wife and I were going to be reinforcing the biases of birth order. All we could do was try to keep the reinforcements positive or at least keep the negative reinforcements to a minimum—a task to which we, reasonably self-aware, college-educated, late-twentieth-century adults with a shelf full of child psychology books and friends we could consult who had sagging shelves of their own, felt equal. We didn't know whether this child of ours would wind up being an only child—in effect a firstborn without a younger sibling—but surely if we could anticipate problems, we could defuse them, all things being equal.

It wasn't until the second child came along that I realized just how unequal things really are—how impossibly unfair and how intractably out of our control. We tried to avoid burdening our child with being the center of a pre-Copernican cosmos, and we failed. And if I ever doubt it, all I have to do is think of the names we chose for our children. For the firstborn, Gabriel—a beautiful name, I think, but undeniably a careful name, an effortful name, a name that seems to show the strain that went into arriving at it. A labor of love, to be sure, but a labor nonetheless. And then there's Charlie. Not the regal Charles or the kick-me-sign Chuck but something casual, in between, tossed off. A name that sounds as if it just happened.

It didn't, of course. In some ways "Charlie" took more work than "Gabriel." My wife and I didn't want to know the sex of our first child until the moment it arrived, as if somehow we could preserve some measure of spontaneity in a procedure that had been marching toward its conclusion for nine months and that we had been anticipating and rehearsing and planning down to the last detail, including this: If it's a boy, it's "Gabriel." But when the second child came along, we had known his sex for four and a half months, and we still didn't have a name. Charles had been one of our options, but it didn't seem right; at some level we must have sensed that it would have sounded as sculpted, as studied as Gabriel. It wasn't until the day after he was born—an entire day of life without a name, a prospect that four years earlier would have scandalized our expanding sense of parental responsibility—that it hit us: Charlie. A compromise.

It wasn't so much that we were less watchful or more permissive toward the second child, as my friend's joke had warned. It wasn't that we had given the question of what to name the second son any less thought than we had for the first. Instead, the difference in our approaches to the two children was that by the time the second son came along, we'd learned that we could proceed under the assumption that it would all work out in the end somehow. Maybe not for the best—that would be too much to hope for—but it would work out nonetheless.

This was a hard lesson to learn. Despite the ample warnings, it was still a revelation, in the first months of Gabriel's life, just how much babies cry. They cry at anything, of course, but then they *keep* crying. We, the adults, try to reason with them: See, we're changing the diaper, rubbing the bump, feeding the emptiness. Certainly we don't expect them to understand that the discomfort will pass; such an understanding would require a knowledge of the linearity of time that they can't possibly have. But for some reason we do expect them to understand that when the discomfort is *leaving* them, when it's *almost* all gone—that surely *now* they can stop crying.

But they don't. And after a while it dawned on me why. Until it *is* completely gone—until the last vestige of the offending, discomfiting experience has vanished—how can the baby know that it is not eternal? The baby cries and keeps on crying because the baby doesn't know that this discomfort or pain or fear won't last forever, that the world hasn't suddenly changed in some fundamental and awful, unbearable, and most of all irreversible way.

In other words, they cry for the same reason their crying unnerves us. It was upon me and a part of me before I knew it, this lesson: A baby's crying frightens us firsttime parents because we don't know it won't last forever. We don't know for certain that *our* lives haven't suddenly changed in some unbearable and irreversible way. This was indeed one of the Mysteries of Parenthood I had heard so much about, something I had to experience in order to understand fully. The rub was that, properly understood, it wasn't a lesson that applied only toward experiences that were painful—that I wished would end.

With Gabriel I hadn't been able to wait for each next stage of development. I had found myself living in a constant tension between fascination with the moment and curiosity about what's next. And when that curiosity became too much—became impatience—I couldn't help exerting a certain pressure to advance to the next stage, to move along, to *get on with it already*. It was just like the crying: What if this stage lasts forever?

Now, there's a distinction between monitoring a behavioral problem, or worrying about a cognitive delay, and actively encouraging advancement—actually imposing our adult will to change an uncomfortable situation in a way that a crying child can't—and I'm sorry to say we didn't respect it. One example will suffice (and even that's almost more than I can bear to repeat). At the age of one and a half, during a routine visit to the pediatrician, Gabriel learned what that hypnotic, spinning, whirring, magical machine in the corner of the doctor's office was called: cen . . . tri . . . fuge. He learned it because my wife and I taught it to him, syllable by syllable. We said it. He said it. We laughed, clapped. He laughed, clapped. Make no mistake: This wasn't an evil, one-sided act of selfishness on our part; but it *was* an act of selfishness. No doubt Gabriel received some gratification from the laughter and applause of his parents. It's just that our gratification was greater than his and certainly a higher priority for us. How a one-and-a-half-year-old's vocabulary could possibly benefit from the addition of "centrifuge" never occurred to us; it was simply satisfaction enough that he could parrot the nonsense syllables.

The temptation to pressure him to advance, to excel, to master tasks for which he couldn't possibly have the least practical use was complicated by the fact that he *was* precocious—that even without our prompting he routinely performed feats beyond his months. We didn't know he could count to ten until the day he did it, on the swing at a playground, reciting along with the mother who was pushing her child on the next swing. (Apparently he'd picked it up from *Sesame Street*.) We didn't know he could read until he suddenly surprised us with the word "no" one afternoon in his stroller, rolling past a street sign. I'm not trying to excuse our behavior; I'm ashamed for my part in it. But I am trying to convey how easy it was to overlook that this pressure was there until it wasn't—until, that is, the arrival of Charlie.

With Gabriel I couldn't wait to see what would happen next; by the time Charlie came along, I knew all too well. I not only recognized each successive stage of development with a delicious jolt of déjà vu, but I realized I now knew exactly what to expect. More to the point, I knew what to *savor*. The place at the back of the scalp where what little hair there is seems to swirl together into one ever-tightening spiral? "The center of the universe," I used to call it on Gabriel (unwittingly establishing even then his eventual Copernican displacement). On Charlie I still called it that, but only to myself because I couldn't bear to say out loud what I knew I was about to lose. And lose it I did. The hair lengthened;

the spiral vanished. Or the cuddling helplessness, the infant's inability to hold up even the head? It was back, too; and then it wasn't. The first focusing on the outside world? The initial halting attempts at nonsense syllables? Here again, and gone again.

If anything, the danger this time was the temptation to exert a constant, if unconscious, pressure on the second child to stay at each stage—to *not* get on with it. I never act on that temptation, I hope, but I would be a fool to deny it's there. *Don't hold your head up. Don't focus. Don't talk. Not now, not yet, because once you do, you'll never be speechless, sightless, powerless again.*

Not that it would matter. There is no stopping Charlie, even if I wanted to, which I don't (however much I do). The universe he finds himself inhabiting with his brother is indeed a distinctly Copernican one. They share a solar system, each following a predictable path in an eternal parade of cause-and-effect perfection. If this, then that. Being *here,* now, implies being *there,* then. Charlie can observe Gabriel and see it's so. He can do the clockwork math as well as Isaac Newton did. "I be big like Gabriel," he told me the other day. "I be seven like Gabriel."

Gabriel, for his part, can do the math as well. It's no coincidence, I think, that the first time he expressed any reservations about getting older was just before his fifth birthday and just after the birth of his brother. It was, as they say, an age-appropriate anxiety, but surely the arrival of Charlie didn't help. Gabriel still wanted his presents; he was quite clear on that point. He just didn't want the birthday that went with them, because, as he also made clear, this whole getting older business eventually came to no good end.

This, then, is our happy hell. We gain paradise, but the price of admission is the foreknowledge of its loss. The firstborn's discovery of his place in the universe is our own. When Charlie cries, it never occurs to me that it might go on forever because now I know it won't, because now I know, in a way I never knew before and with a certainty that was inconceivable to me until I enrolled in the Parenthood, *he* won't. A mixed blessing, at best, this insight.

One day not long ago, sitting on a bench in the Central Park Zoo, I was thinking about the question of birth order while waiting for Gabriel and Charlie to finish their ice cream—or, more accurately, while Charlie and I waited for Gabriel to finish his. Charlie already had handed his strawberry bar over to me, having eaten only half of it but figuring, correctly, that there would always be more where that came from. Gabriel, however, was doing with his chocolate bar what he usually did with ice cream; licking it slowly, prolonging the experience, refusing to abandon it until he had finished every last drop—figuring, equally correctly, that its moment was fleeting. I mentioned to Gabriel that I had been thinking about when he was born and how he had kept his eyes closed for the first few days. He thought about this for a while, and I could see him drifting somewhere. I knew that look. I also knew to wait. After all, what could possibly be the hurry? When he came back, he said, "I was scared of the new world, I guess."

That would be my guess, too.

A Second Chance at Childhood

ROB SPILLMAN

*F*our years ago when my wife became pregnant, I felt a rush of a giddy bravado. I had created life, I was going to be a father. The godlike aura faded halfway through a celebratory martini when I choked on the proverbial bitter cocktail olive of self-doubt. How could I possibly be a parent when I myself was never a child? What did I know about children? This fear rode herd on a pack of ugly insecurities and anxieties: fear of failing my child, of not being able to connect emotionally or love him or her unconditionally. Intellectually I knew I wanted the experience of raising a child, and this emotionally detached desire scared me. I wondered if it was the same feeling my parents possessed when they decided to have a child. Like my parents, I was driven to succeed as an artist. My parents, both professional musicians, had single-mindedly pursued their ambition, and I had simply been along for the ride, witnessing the dedication needed to succeed. At times I felt more like the product of their collaboration, the composition of a piece of music, than a child.

Ever since I could speak, both of my parents preached that I could be anything I wanted as long as I was willing to make sacrifices and dedicate myself solely to work as they had. Now, as a man, I felt a similar drive to succeed. What would happen when I found myself in the condition of, in

Raymond Carver's words, "unrelieved responsibility and permanent distraction"? Equally strong and equally worrisome was the strange sense of desperately wanting something else from life, something I had never experienced. All I did know was that I was determined to give my kid a real childhood. I never wanted him or her to feel like an afterthought to my work. If I was truly lucky and I could balance my work with fatherhood while attempting to steer around the various domestic and personal land mines that blew up my parents' lives, maybe I would succeed at both.

My few early memories are as scattered and random as my peripatetic childhood. The background for the ordinary divorce story was Berlin, where I attended a trilingual school where everyone spoke at least French, German, and English. After the split I lived mostly with my father, a concert pianist. I spent summers backstage at the music festivals of Chautauqua, New York, and Aspen, Colorado, with long solo plane flights to New Orleans where my mother, an opera singer, had fled after my father came out of the closet. My non-musical memories are fuzzy—the gritty feel of a sandbox behind a large creaky house in one of the neighborhoods where we once lived in Berlin; the bitter stench of onion soup, served at midnight in the ornate basement of a gilded concert hall in some medieval European city where my father had just finished performing; invisible under my father's practice-room piano as I felt the vibrations of a Schuman sonata; the muffled, safe sounds as I swam below the surface of the murky water of Lake Chautauqua; watching small green lizards clinging to my mother's windows in New Orleans, stubbornly suctioned to the glass no matter how hard I pulled on them.

My autobiographical slide show becomes much more detailed the closer the images are to the stage, the place behind which I spent most of my childhood. The costume crates, racks of stage sets and props, and afterward the all-night cast parties where I'd sip ginger ale alongside champagne-swilling drama queens of every age, gender, and sexuality while Joni Mitchell impersonators draped themselves over the piano and some baritone in eyeliner put the moves on a chubby chorus girl. When I tell people about my unusual upbringing, they invariably say that I must have had a fabulous and glamorous childhood. Fabulous, sure; glamorous, sometimes; but there was very little opportunity to be a "child." As soon as the school day was over, I was whisked over to a music conservatory, a practice room, or a concert hall, places where I rarely saw other children. These were arenas of concentration and art, where little boys were not supposed to be little boys. I entertained myself by exploring catwalks, light towers, subbasements, set shops, and prop rooms, an Eloise in the opera house. I remember only a few games—chess with my parents' students and fellow musicians, hearts and spades on the long solo flights with stewardesses and pilots, and Boggle with my father on our one- or two-week vacation between the end of a school year and the start of summer school. I had no way of knowing that I was missing Tom and Jerry, marbles, or GI Joes. In the presence of other children, my lack of most common kid touch-points rendered me mute and awkward, like an alien landed for a quick, observational visit. All the other kids seemed to have lived wherever we were forever, and they had so many things that I couldn't relate to—siblings, longtime friends, and the common language and rituals of childhood.

I was certain that once I was confronted with a child, even my own child—or, perhaps, especially my own child—my complete lack of any real cohesive childlike experience would once again pitch me into that withdrawn persona. I would feel like a stranger, an outsider in my own parent-child relationship, and I would shut down, as I had in the past when confronted with the possibility of emotional pain.

It sounds clichéd and it sounds phony, but the second I held my daughter in the sterile, freezing confines of a hospital birthing room, all doubts about my ability to love evaporated. My fear was obliterated by a new desire: to protect my child, to learn to understand her, and, in the process, scary as it was, to let myself become vulnerable. For months I had prepared for this day by reading every parenting and child psychology book I could find, from *Daddying for Dummies* to *Psychomotor Control in Newborns*. I was ready to change diapers, chart growth patterns, and stimulate those budding rods and cones. I was ready to give. What I was beginning to understand was that I was also ready to receive. I had no idea how desperately I wanted, maybe needed, to be a father.

It soon became clear that only in hindsight do we dissect and judge our childhoods. Unlike adults, babies are pretty forgiving. Their expectations are simple. Having godlike power over such an impressionable creature gave me an embarrassing rush of confidence. I fed her and she stopped crying. I rocked her and she smiled. Still, I didn't trust myself with infant-specific things. Instead of *Goodnight Moon,* I lulled Isadora to sleep with *The Collected Poems of Elizabeth Bishop.* After this success I became bolder. If Isadora smiled or cooed at "Itsy Bitsy Spider," then I kept singing it. If she howled over "Rock-a-bye Baby," I put it in mental storage and improvised "Yellow Submarine" or "God Save the Queen." And as she got older and acquired verbal sophistication, I found myself meeting her on a common level. I became freer in trying out "childish" things—Play-Doh, finger paints, face painting. And my mistakes—confusing Prairie Dawn with Betty Lou, not understanding that sweet Bavarian-looking Playmobil people have awful tempers, botching paper dolls so they looked like the Manson girls—didn't stick with Isadora. What stuck was a consistency of affection, a feeling of being at the center of the parental universe.

She fed me what no one else ever could. Even my wife, who had done wonders in drawing me out, didn't love me as unconditionally as my daughter. Before she could even speak, Isadora seemed to be saying, "C'mon, Dad, get on the floor and we'll figure things out together." She didn't care that I had to learn all the nursery rhymes, that I had never played ring-around-a-rosy. She didn't notice that we were both experiencing the joy of childhood for the first time.

While I was relishing my daughter's childhood and these feelings of unconditional love, I was also aware that the floodgates holding back a vast reservoir of anger and resentment were being seriously battered. I wanted memories of finger painting, riding bikes, and playing in the leaves with my parents, memories I didn't have. And after my daughter's birth, I found it difficult to watch my parents being doting grandparents. Where was this when I was her age?

Yet as I try to finish various writing projects while juggling outings to the zoo, playground, and birthday parties, I also now empathize more with what they had gone through. How overwhelming and difficult it must have been to be single parents isolated from friends and family, trying to forge careers in a brutal field, while both of them were dealing with my father's newfound sexuality. And all of this without adequate emotional equipment. Each came from frigid midwestern families where affection was rarely if ever shown, even to sensitive, artistic children. Isadora, by contrast, lives with two parents who have been together for twelve years and who are still finding new ways of being in love. We have also made the decision not to uproot and are writers who have the luxury of working at home so that we can be with Isadora during the day.

My greatest professional fear—that I would not have enough time to write and that I would be ragged and unfocused—has turned out to be staggeringly unfounded. Because I have opened myself up to a much greater emotional range, I find that my work has also opened up. While the actual physical time at the computer has decreased, my output has increased and my focus, resolve, and discipline are stronger than before Isadora was born.

I recently came across a picture of myself taken when I was the same age as Isadora is now. Though physically I resemble her in some ways— the pouty lower lip, the wide-open eyes—I have never seen her with a similar expression. In the crisp black-and-white photo I am sitting in a straight-backed chair, a book on my lap, a blank, lost look on my face. Not only do I seem adrift, but I seem vulnerable, scared, damaged. I will do whatever it takes so that my daughter never wears the same expression.

But is that realistic? I can't hope to shield her from all emotional pain, and I don't want to. I am very aware of the dangers of overcompensating for my own childhood. It's a struggle not to smother, and it's also a struggle not to be simply her playmate. She doesn't need me to be a friend; she needs me to be a father—which is harder and scarier, much more of a minefield of potential disasters and disappointments.

I am lucky in that I have a daughter who has let me grow up with her. I can only wonder at how good I would feel about being a father if she hadn't been such a verbal, affectionate kid. And I wonder if I might have been less willing to give or receive love if she had been a he. I think I would have looked for myself much more in a boy, constantly searching for traces of that damaged boy in the picture. I would have feared that he'd judge me, afraid he'd know me as I knew myself. If he had been as joyful as Isadora, I wonder if I would have resented his happiness. I could see myself childishly displacing my anger onto him for having a conventional, happy childhood. And there was probably a subconscious feeling that little girls need more affection and protection than little boys—who, like me, can fend for themselves even if they end up repressed and angry. I nursed these dark thoughts right up until the moment in the delivery room when our doctor yelled, "It's a girl."

Now, three years later, as I write this—three years of struggling with the anger and with the pain of the past slowly dragged out into the light—I'm trying to stare down an amniocentesis test. I'm going to be the father of a boy. Were the last three years just a warm-up for the real test? I don't think so. Isadora and my wife have patiently allowed me to develop as a father. Now I am once again plunging into the unknown. As an only child, I am eager to vicariously experience my children's lives as siblings. I know nothing about raising a son, but three years ago I knew nothing about raising a daughter. There is only one thing I am certain of—my son, like Isadora, will have a childhood completely different from mine. And with Isadora's help he will be as curious, affectionate, and loved as a child can be. This is my vow and my prayer.

PART II

ROOM TO GROW

Just the One

ALICE ELLIOTT DARK

He is asleep as his father and I begin the day. We don't have to tip-toe around or lower our voices; nothing can wake him except a bad dream. I can even go into his room and put the laundry away.

"I love it when he first wakes up," I tell my mother. "He makes the same faces and stretches that he did as a baby. Were any of us like that?"

She shrugs. "I don't know. There was such a rush in the morning to get you all out the door. It was a blur."

My son can't be a blur; he's an "only" child. When he's in the house, I know what he's doing at every moment. I never find him in a different room than I imagined or discover he's drifted into a nap when I thought he was playing. He's threaded into my consciousness so deeply that I can't think without somehow evoking him. It's not that I'm an unusually atten-tive mother. I think it's a combination of our personalities and the fact that nothing has come between us since his birth. I rarely have to take anyone's side against him or divide my child-time so that he gets less. No, he's not a blur—but should he be? Would it be better for all of us if he weren't the "only" one?

* * *

I didn't plan to have only one child. When I was little, I loved large families, the bigger the better. I was drawn to books that featured boisterous broods. A title like *The Happy Hollisters,* with its suggestion of family fun, was enough to keep me in my room on even the clearest beach afternoon, reading and fantasizing. My best friend had six in her family, two more than me, and other families I knew were even larger. I loved the feeling in those houses of endless company, kids everywhere, kids and their things, pets, buddies. There was always something to do and someone to do it with. In contrast to television where the parents knew best and ran their broods with military efficiency and ministerial benevolence, the kids essentially ruled. Parents seemed able to maintain a close level of involvement up to a ratio of two to one (child to parent), but when it went beyond that—if there were three or more kids to each adult in the house—the dynamic shifted, the parents faded, and the children prevailed in spite of any amount of rules that had been set to control them. There was power in numbers. If Carol and Mike Brady hadn't had Alice, they'd have been in serious trouble. That seems to be the case across the board.

You could get lost in a big family, too—lost in a good way. The kids seemed freer, less observed. When they got in trouble, a number of them were apt to be punished at once, or else the parents were too overwhelmed to do much about the crime at hand. When they did get together as a group, they often had fun in intriguing ways; for example, they might cook up a performance, like the Von Trapp family in *The Sound of Music.* And in big families the station wagons always filled up to the point where a few kids had to sit in the way back. Dibs! At some point in my childhood I decided I'd have thirteen children, a big happy family. Surprise, surprise, life didn't work out like that.

Just the One

*   *   *

He wakes up.

"Family sandwich!" my husband calls out, and the two of us jump on our son's bed and squeeze him between us.

"Uh oh," he says with a giggle.

After a minute he slides free and heads off toward his own day. My husband and I still lie there, recapturing, for a moment, our couplehood. As if sensing this defection, our child makes a dramatic reappearance.

"Come on, guys!" he says. "You're the ones who always tell me I stall in the mornings!"

My husband and I glance at each other, a look filled with a combination of resignation (we have wrought this), nostalgia (we used to *talk* to each other), and amusement (he's got our number!). It took a while to adjust to being a threesome, but that's what we are now. With an only child, the marriage stretches and never gets to snap back as the numbers begin to balance out. There is no category of "the children" in our household. There is just *us*.

He tugs our hands.

"Come on, guys. We have to get going."

And so *we* start our day.

*   *   *

Suburbia is packed with children. The days of being socially responsible by having one child or two at most appear to be well over. There are three kindergarten classes at my son's elementary school this year, over eighty children, but there were only twelve slots available for new students. The rest were taken by siblings of children already in the school, who have first priority. At pickup time in the afternoon, the schoolyard is thronged with toddlers and women carrying newborns in portable infant car seats. There is an astonishing number of twins. Everyone jokes about the lack of sex happening in the bedrooms of parents of ankle-biters, but clearly something is going on.

When I make new acquaintances and divulge the information that I have only this one seven-year-old to care for, I am liable to get one of the following responses:

"You're lucky. You can't imagine how much harder it gets with two and three—forget it."

"No wonder you have time to write."

"Are you planning another?"

"It's not too late. I read about a sixty-three-year-old woman who had a perfectly healthy baby."

"Well, you can always adopt. My neighbor has an adopted daughter from China, and she's great."

"Don't you worry about him being spoiled?"

"I can't imagine not having a constant playmate around. Do you have to play with him yourself?"

What can I say? Yes, no, thanks for the tip, but unless something un-foreseen happens, he's going to be our only child. I utter the phrase re-luctantly, angry with myself for falling into the idiom that I've come to resent. *Only.* It is a lash and I feel the sting of it. Only implies a problem. Scarcity. Distress. A lack, alack. It implies that my son is not enough and that I'm somehow less of a mother than the women who move around town with one in the Snugli, one in the stroller, and one or two more traipsing alongside. As with every aspect of parenthood, people can be as judgmental about the composition of a small family (selfish and cowardly) as they are of a large one (selfish and ignorant). I don't know how to defend myself against the charge that something is missing in my life, because part of me agrees. I am missing something. But would more children take that feeling away?

I don't think so. This missing feeling is like homesickness, that strange kind of homesickness where you long for a place you never lived, a family unknown to you. But should the quest to satisfy that longing take the most literal form? Of course I have curiosity about what another child might be like, but wouldn't I feel that again? I know women with five kids who would have more if they could afford it. People with all boys are wistful for a girl, and vice versa. My friends who are nearing forty are grieving over the coming end of choice in the matter; whether or not they want more children, they hate having the option cut off. As for our own greener grass, my husband and I would love to have a daughter. I'd welcome a second chance to see what results would come of improving on the mistakes I've made with our son. It would be interesting to see how another boy would differ from the first. And I'd really enjoy having that easy, sleeps-and-eats, cuddly second baby I've seen around town. But for a variety of reasons—primarily financial—my husband and I have decided our family is complete as is. Whatever we are missing, we have to let go. We are hurried along in this process by knowing that as each stage of childhood passes, it is over for us. Yet it is hard to mourn for very long; something else is always going on.

* * *

"I really love Aiden," my son tells me at breakfast. Aiden is the little brother of his best friend. "And Charlotte. And Eden, too."

I am pleased he is so full of love, that he cares for little children, but I also feel guilty that I haven't provided him with a baby sibling of his own. "And they love you," I say.

"And I love Justin. Really, he's just so great. I'd take a bullet for him if anyone tried to shoot him."

He is flushed with his own heroism. I'm shaken that he knows phrases like 'take a bullet" and that he can conceive of his friend being shot, but I let it go. It is important that he has figured out a way to expand his circle.

"Why don't we buy a big house with the Wrights?" he suggests. "Wouldn't that be great?"

He is so much like me; he, too, wants that big happy family. But I had three siblings and, in time, eight stepbrothers and -sisters. The bodies were there, but I couldn't make them act like *Little House on the Prairie*. It won't do any good to tell him this, though. The longing is one that goes deep, and he'll have to figure out for himself how to deal with it.

"Maybe we can go on a vacation with them sometime," I say.

"Yay!" He forms a high fist and yanks it down to his waist in the current gesture of triumph. He knows we're not going to live with the Wrights or anybody but each other. Nevertheless, he likes to dream. I did that, too, for hours and hours. George Harrison, the Beatle, was my brother for years. My son has told me he'd like a slightly older Korean brother who knows tae kwan do. I tell him he can have that brother in the same way I had George. He can fantasize, pretend. He can learn to fill in his own gaps, to prepare himself for being grown up.

Just the One

*   *   *

I've done some research on the subject of only children. Recent studies suggest that they do as well as any other children, perhaps slightly better in the areas of verbal sophistication and maturity. As adults they are liable to be exceptionally successful. They aren't necessarily lonely, nor do they miss out on the aspects of development that involve negotiating with other children, because kids are among their peers for hours and hours daily. In other words, the aura of blight that surrounded only children when I was young simply doesn't pan out in any discernible ways.

This is all good news, but I need more reassurances, so I continually conduct an informal research. The adults I know who were only children admit to wishing they had siblings, but the fantasy always involved a soul mate, a pure ally, a *Little Women* kind of closeness, not a flesh-and-blood creature who might torment and dominate. A few are glad they were solo and wouldn't have had it any other way. What disturbs them most is the idea that they will be alone after their parents die. With living siblings there's a chance of sharing the burden, of family life continuing on. We all long for connection. From my observation it seems that the older people get, the more they seek out their blood relatives and search for anchors in their specific families and pasts. This is definitely going to be harder for my son than for others. He will have to go further to create a sense of extended family. I try to help by making plans with the cousins as often as possible.

For now, he considers the animals who live with us his kin. "I have two cat sisters, one dog sister, and one cat brother," he is apt to say. People are quick to tell him that you can't have a house pet for a sibling, but

I'm pleased he feels that way. The more of the world he feels related to, the better. I hope he will find a way to create a satisfying family for himself in some form or another. From his point of view, the world seems big and promising. I am glad of that, although I can't feel it; for me, most of the time, the universe weighs forty-three pounds.

* * *

I have a lot of fears, ranging from the generic—What if something happens to him?—to a horrifying specificity: What if he is kidnapped or gets a disease or is hit by a car? This is, to me, the worst aspect of having an only child—the knowledge that, if he dies, the devastation will be complete. Whenever I read about people who lose a child, they are likely to say that the only thing that kept them going was having to take care of their other children still alive. What reason is there to go on if you lose your only child? For myself, I can't imagine. The only thing I can think of is that I do know pain lifts and that it is possible to have a relationship with the dead. I don't know if that would be enough for me, though. When I consider the prospect of my son being killed, I want to die with him. I pray that nothing will happen to him; I don't know who I'd be.

* * *

"Things don't always work out the way you imagine," I tell my son when he asks why I don't have another baby.

We have our most risky talks in the car. In the rearview mirror I see him looking out the window, considering.

"At least you got to have one kid," he says finally.

"The best kid."

"You're just saying that."

His remark is light and teasy, but I explain anyway: Even if I had other kids, I'd still adore him, et cetera.

"I know, Mom. You already told me."

He's right. I've told him and he has believed me; he has no issue here. But I go on.

"It would be fun to have more kids just like you," I say.

"But then I'd be jealous," he says.

"So you don't want a brother anymore?" I'm leading the witness. It's wrong, I know it, but I also want to know what he's thinking.

"An older brother," he says. "One who wouldn't mess up my stuff."

"I don't think that's going to happen," I say.

"I know. That's okay. I like our family."

"I like *you*," I tell him.

There is a pause as we bask in our mutual admiration society. He senses an opening.

"Hey, I have an idea. Can we get a video?" he asks.

"Sure."

We roam the aisles, examining the boxes, and finally settle on *Air Force One*. He has seen it before, but no one tires quickly of Harrison Ford.

"I just wish the kid in it was a boy," he says.

I deliver the standard parental response: "You can't have everything."

But as he drifts over to the gum ball machine and examines it as if it fell from heaven, I think maybe I do.

Befriending Zoé

HILARY SELDEN ILLICK

Before I became a parent, I worked as an elementary school teacher. While I liked a lot of the parents, even became good friends with some, I was struck by how, on the topic of their child, they tended to become a little disturbed. Their energy shifted perceptibly. Jaws tightened, neck veins filled up and bulged out. They talked a little faster, edged forward on their seats. Even when offering up a light anecdote, laughing in a loving way about something their child did or said, they often became noticeably agitated. Parents would stop me to ask dire questions about perfectly normal children, questions like "Do any of the other kids like Amy? She never means to be as rude as she is," or "Ben is so painfully shy—does he ever say *a word?*" The intensity of the parents' concern bewildered me at the time. Don't you guys have careers? I sometimes wanted to ask. Interests? Hobbies? Friends of your own?

Fragments of conversations replay in my mind, a decade later. A parent myself now, I can see how oblivious I was to the power that I, as the teacher, possessed with these poor people. I had no idea that with a single offhand comment I could determine the tenor of their day, even influence the way they viewed their own child. "How did he behave?" a mother would ask me at pickup time, her face stricken, held in torturous suspense. "Derek didn't hit anybody today, did he?" And I, single, in my twenties, unaware of the way each elapsed second made the interaction more unbearable for the mother, would look upward, scanning the sky leisurely as I reviewed the day. "Oh, yup," I'd respond at last. "He did hit, actually; he hit Peter. And Lars. Peter at math time, Lars on the swings." My reports were candid, offered neutrally, because the thing was, it never struck me as pathological that Derek hit. Others hit, too. Some screamed. Some cried. One, whenever she giggled, peed torrentially in her pants. Even the one that year who bit seemed well within the bounds of normal. She was a kid, after all, a little feisty girl who, when she got frustrated, opened her jaws. Of course these behaviors needed to be addressed; we were all working in the spirit of socializing these kids. But it seemed inevitable to me that they would grow into more or less reasonable adults. I still remember my own perplexity at the sight of Derek's mother as she drove away, slouched with defeat over her white-knuckled clench of the steering wheel. I had no idea that someday that same posture would be mine, that at a preschool potluck I'd find myself slumped over a mini picnic table painted primary blue, at the nadir of my parenting experience.

*   *   *

The potluck marked the end of the year for the Back Yarders, the class of four-year-olds soon to be graduated from this preschool, bound for kindergarten. As far as I was concerned, it had been a trying year. My daughter Zoé had played inseparably with her three best friends—Elijah, Bess, and Tory—day after day, month after month, sharing a communal rapport best described as litigious. Incendiary. Divorce court. Anything but carefree. Early on I had learned, out of self-preservation, to avoid asking, "How did Zoé's day go?" But even so, it seemed rare that I made it in and out of that place at pickup time without being spotted by the Back Yard teacher and summoned over for a little tête-à-tête. The words, "Could I speak to you for a moment?" became my most dreaded phrase.

Zoé and her three friends had spent their Back Yard year playing with—which translates directly into "haggling over"—an extensive set of miniature plastic dogs, stored above the blocks shelf in the center of the classroom. This is California. With the exception of two dark and stormy months we call the rainy season, the weather tends to be accommodating, inviting for outdoor play. But the haggling foursome seldom made it out into fresh air. They stayed inside on the rug, excluding other children as they constructed out of blocks elaborate dynasties for their miniature plastic canines, bickering tirelessly over (for some reason adults could never fathom) the much adored West Highland white terrier and the coveted Lhasa apso. They could deflect even the most diplomatic adult attempts at conflict resolution. When the teacher proposed that each child take a five-minute turn with the special dogs, Zoé would come back with, "Why not six?"

The day before the potluck had been Sports Day, the annual Back Yard field trip to the playground for a morning of fun and organized games. Zoé, Elijah, Bess, and Tory, I was informed at pickup time, never made it onto the playing fields. They bickered on the sidelines over who would cover which base in softball, who would get to wear the shin guards in soccer, who would be on whose team. The entire class returned to the preschool muddied and flush-faced. But only for Zoé and Co. were the mud, sweat, and grass stains a result of melodramatically throwing themselves to the ground during verbal disputes. I did not take the news of Sports Day well. It felt for me like the final crushing blow after a year of crushing blows, irrefutable evidence that all was not well with our child, that she was not progressing as she should, that I, as the mother, held primary blame. I could think and speak of little else.

My husband, Pierre, suggested that I might be overreacting. When I think back on it now, with the benefit of more than a year's distance, I imagine that neither the content nor the tone of what Zoé's teacher said were loaded with the negative wallop I perceived then. But the experience of being called aside by the teacher felt like electroshock. I'm sure I barely listened. That Zoé had another rocky morning said to me only one thing: Zoé had somehow caused problems in the classroom, had failed to meet a social expectation—and, as the person spearheading the movement to socialize her, so had I. The preschool was a parent co-op, where each morning four or five parents participated alongside the teacher, meeting at noon to discuss the salient events of the day. Because of their frequent conflicts, the names of Zoé and her friends came up often in these meetings—which I took, in this small community, as tantamount to being affixed with a child-sized sort of scarlet letter.

I had tried, throughout the year, doing role-plays at home with Zoé: A little girl finds herself quarreling with her friends; the little girl says, "I need a break," and leaves the group to serenely page through a book. I'd invited other children over for play dates, carefree children whose breeziness, I hoped, would rub off on Zoé. But no matter how well any such play date went, once back in school, Zoé walked right past these happy-go-lucky children as if they weren't even there. She headed straight for Elijah, Bess, and Tory, with their oppositional tendencies and sophisticated verbal skills. By the time I heard about Sports Day, I knew the jury was finally in: Pierre and I had raised an antisocial kid.

"Come on, Hil," Pierre reasoned. "Don't you know deep down that

Zoé's fine? That even if she never participated in a single organized event for the rest of her life, she'd still be an incredible person?"

"I'm at the point," I said, "where I just want to hear that Zoé had a great day. I want to pick her up from school and have someone just say, 'Wow! What a terrific kid!' "

"But why? Why do you need to hear that so badly? Can't *you* decide she's a terrific kid, no matter what anyone else says or feels?"

While I admired Pierre's loyalty, his integrity, his inviolable sense of himself in the world, a sense that included his daughter and could not be damaged by the opinions of others, I sometimes thought the guy was from another planet. We had been through many versions of this conversation before, even before we had children, when we were discussing my Fear of Judgment from the Outer World, but I just couldn't revolutionize myself to feel the way he did. I wanted to. His way of being looked pretty nice to me. But I could not fabricate out of what felt like thin air a solid, positive, impregnable sense of myself that could weather the negative opinions of others, and now, I was discovering, I could not do it for Zoé either.

I assumed that at least some of the parents of the other Dog-Fixated Excluders would be feeling as mortified as I. At the end-of-the-year potluck, I sought them out. Elbow to elbow, Pierre and I squeezed around the little blue picnic table with the parents of Elijah, Bess, and Tory, balancing paper plates on our laps to make enough room. Here we all were, parents of children who the day before had not made it out onto the fields for a single moment of Sports Day. These other parents, they could not all be taking the news as evenly as Pierre.

But it turned out they could. They were. They did.

Our conversations—interrupted frequently by our children, who ran around without consuming a single calorie of the potluck supper, shrieking, playing, and, yes, haggling over the tire swing—never strayed far from the subject of our four Back Yarders and of the many rows they caused all year long. But the other parents, I noticed, were able to laugh. Able to eat. To go back for seconds of three-bean casserole. Of course no one *loved* the fact that our children were such squabblers. Mention of the countless disputes over that little plastic West Highland white terrier caused these mothers and fathers to roll their eyes. But they were at peace with it, I could tell. Bess's father even went so far as to *praise* the very tendencies that mortified me. "I'm telling you," he said, waving his red plastic fork in the air, "they're budding courtroom lawyers. Believe me, Bess will argue in front of the Supreme Court one day." It's true that his neck veins did bulge out when he said this, the extra blood flow of inflated pride. Like the parents I remembered from my teaching days, his sense of his daughter was a little extreme. But his distortion loomed toward the positive end of the continuum, whereas mine, the other pole. I would have traded places with him before you could say Lhasa apso.

* * *

Shame is not an emotion I have been quick to claim. My experience with the word came from gym classes as a girl, where, whenever one of us did something wrong, the P.E. teacher would shout, "SHAME! NAUGHTY! BAD: SAY IT!" And the whole class of girls would have to shout in unison, "SHAME! NAUGHTY! BAD!" (This happened at least once or twice every gym period, and I wonder now what kind of infractions we were so frequently committing. Not tying our cleats properly? Forgetting to wear bloomers under our pinnies?) Even then I knew that to shout such a phrase was perverse, and I came to see the word *shame* as reserved for usage only by the abject, the extreme, like hard-core Catholics and sadistic gym teachers. I did not understand that shame could live in an average, religiously neutral person like me.

At that Back Yard potluck, however, surrounded by people who, like my own husband, were in their own way giving their kid the benefit of the doubt, I was struck by the sudden awareness of my own shame. Pierre's reaction was not abnormal; *mine* was. Consumed by my own Fear of Judgment, worried only about myself and how the situation reflected on me, I had emotionally distanced myself from my own child. I had acted precisely like the kind of person I feared most: someone who stood back and judged Zoé without curiosity or compassion. Riding home from the potluck, I hung my head.

Once I acknowledged my shame over giving the negative opinions of others far more clout than the fiber of one of the most important and enduring relationships I will ever have, I began to notice the presence of shame on other levels. In fact, I came to understand what probably should have been obvious from the start: that I felt ashamed of the way Zoé acted. I did not know, I really didn't, that my horrible anxiety and my inability to stand still and at peace while listening to her teacher (or another parent) describe Zoé's behavior were caused by shame. Zoé haggled. She refused to give people what they wanted. She asked for more than she was offered and wanted what she did not have. I began to understand that I was ashamed about the facets of my own character that I saw reflected in Zoé, characteristics of myself that I had tried hard to deny. When I was a teacher, I observed this phenomenon over and over. It seemed as though every time a parent could not tolerate something about his or her own child, that parent possessed the same trait in spades. But the parent never seemed aware of the parallel. Parents who came to talk to me about their child's intolerable habit of interrupting invariably cut me off when I started to respond. Parents of whiny children whined about their child's tendency to whine. I thought about printing up a bumper sticker: WHAT YOU CANNOT STAND ABOUT YOUR CHILD, YOU *REALLY* CANNOT STAND ABOUT YOURSELF. I did not have children myself at the time and so could afford to be a little glib.

My parents had not intended to shame me. They brought their children up in the late sixties and seventies with the goal of endowing them with healthy self-esteem. Countless times a day they told us how great we were, and they meant it. But despite their best intentions, I came away from my childhood with the message that I was supposed to be easily satisfied, breezy company, amenable to whatever came my way. Of course I am not like that at all, but I have spent a long time pretending. I am not the winsome hitchhiker along for the carefree ride of life that I always believed I should be, someone with no specific demands about where and how to go, and entertaining stories to tell. Perhaps that blithe hitchhiker was my updated version of the 1950s hostess ideal, the smiling young woman with her white gloves and tea trolley, offering up light and charming anecdotes, unruffled by red wine spilled on a white carpet or uninvited guests. I am much more difficult and complicated and inflexible than either of them, the hitchhiker or the hostess. But I could not have said this or accepted it as easily as I can now had Zoé not spent the fourth year of her life riveted to three argumentative playmates and a shelf of plastic dogs.

Early in my marriage I had to initiate the process of separating my identity from Pierre's. Like Zoé, Pierre does not perceive it as his responsibility to be a social lubricant, which I do. Pierre has been known to pick up a newspaper in the middle of someone's telling him a story. Slowly I've had to learn to see him as a separate individual and hope that the world will, too. At the Back Yard potluck, my need to separate from Zoé as I had from my husband became markedly clear. Because I am her mother, her behavior obviously bears more of a reflection on me than Pierre's—but Zoé's nature is still her own. When it comes right down to it, she gets final say on how she'll act. When Zoé asks someone if they brought her more than the tiny trinket she has just unwrapped, this does not shine the spotlight of bad manners directly on me. What I can do is try to instill in Zoé the social conventions I believe to be worthwhile (like saying, "Thank you," whether she likes the present or not). Yet the more important work for me lies in defusing the emotional charge I experience whenever Zoé (or Pierre) commits what I consider a social faux pas.

As a new mother, I loved Zoé so much I could barely tear myself away from her. I took her everywhere, even to graduate school when I couldn't make other arrangements, nursing her in the sling while sitting in class. It did not occur to me that sometime in Zoé's life I might not approve of her; my approval, like my wonder, respect, and fidelity, seemed infinite. During her first year, though, I began to notice a distinction between when she and I were alone, in our moony swoony togetherness, versus when she and I were in the company of someone I perceived to be judgmental. When I sensed that a friend or baby-sitter or relative was judging Zoé negatively—for clinging too much, usually, and not being able to sit in that person's lap instead of mine—I grew very torn. I suffered what I now understand as a terrible breach of loyalty, giving priority to what this other person seemed to want or need or think, over what I knew would make Zoé most comfortable. In some kind of automatic, unthinking way, I was by extension now doing to Zoé what I had learned

over time to do to myself. When I think back to baby Zoé, her head a perfectly bald sphere, and the way she would reach her dimpled hands toward me, the person she knew best and in whose lap she felt a longing
and a right to be, and I recall that I pushed her away, pushed her back toward our guest, trying to make Zoé do for this other person what I felt
was my job—make them feel comfortable and wanted—I experience a
distinct kind of heartbreak.

*   *   *

It is not as if this magically stopped happening. It is not as if at that
Back Yard potluck a dramatic gong sounded and the challenge I experience with Zoé forever evaporated. Zoé is six now, and even at such a
golden stage in her development, it does still happen that I hear of something she has said or done to someone else or witness the exchange myself, and I cringe. I experience the impulse to whip over to her with my
white gloves and tea trolley to tell her to "be nice." But something way
down in me has grown more tolerant of itself, and the turmoil I experience over Zoé has significantly diminished.

Yesterday evening, during an unexpected heat wave, our neighbor
Rosalinde dropped by and offered to take Zoé and her four-year-old sister to the lake. On their way out, I took Zoé aside—which I did not feel
the need to do with Esmé, who happens to spout a natural font of grati-
tude from her heart. "Please," I urged Zoé, "please, at the lake, be polite."
Zoé, clad in her swimsuit, towel draped around her neck, assured me
that she would. "Of course, Mom," she said, air whistling through the gap
from her missing two front teeth. But when they returned, I could hear
them out in the driveway, Esmé saying thank you, offering Rosalinde a

hug. And Zoé did not say anything. I could hear the momentum gathering in the silence, could almost *hear* that Zoé's hands were probably on her hips. "Rosalinde," Zoé began, "since that snack bar at the lake was closed, can we have dessert at your house?" I felt compelled to run out there and say to Zoé, "No one promised you anything about a *snack bar!*" And say to our neighbor, "Rosalinde, thank you. What Zoé means is 'Thank you.' " But I could not. Lucky for Zoé, I have newborn twins and these days am often pinned to the sofa, nursing the babies in tandem, which has forced me to intervene less in her interactions. I do not rush in and make explanations for Zoé as often as I still feel inclined to, and to my relief I notice that people actually don't tend to take umbrage. Zoé is not that powerful or rude or offensive—not the demon I at one time feared myself to be. "What a good idea, Zoé," I heard Rosalinde respond. "Have you girls ever heard of the ice cream flavor *Neopolitan?*"

Reading to Brendan

TONY EPRILE

"And again. Read it again just one more time, and that's enough!"

This is our nightly ritual. Whichever book I read to Brendan has to be read twice before he'll consent to having the light turned off, a kiss and a hug and that's good night. It's not the individual book or books that matter but the ceremony itself. There is an enormous power in the repetition of a story, a liturgical quality once satisfied by attendance at church or sabbath services but largely lacking in the distractions of contemporary life.

After chewing his fluoridated vitamin, having his teeth brushed, and throwing the two decorative pillows and all the stuffed animals off the bed, Brendan climbs in beneath his Winnie the Pooh bedsheets, and I lie down next to him to read whatever book he has chosen. The storytelling is not a simple transferring of information but a process that engages all the senses. No matter how wild he was moments before—jumping on his mattress trampoline-style, pushing my head off the pillow mischievously—once we start reading there is a sinking into calm. Our muscles relax and grow heavy. Brendan squirms for a moment or two and then finds just the right spot on my shoulder to rest his head. I read aloud to his soft sighs, his gradually slower and more audible breathing, the sun-baked pigeon odor of a little boy's hair.

Clackety clack—clackety clack
There was a big train

The rhythm of the spoken words lulls us both into a soporific state, a combination of profound relaxation and concentrated attention. It is a deeply sensory experience: the little room in the half-darkness of a single lamp, the clean, warm smell of a well-cared-for but energetic child, the relaxed, trustful small body, the sound of words gradually unfolding into a story . . .

and clickety click—clickety click—clickety click
There was a very little train.

I read to Brendan every night. I read to him not because it's my responsibility or because it's good for him but because I enjoy it. There is so much written for parents about how important it is that you read to your child, how being read to makes children's brains grow and increases their I.Q. We live in a utilitarian—and fearful—age; we're supposed to do things with our children because these things are *of use,* they teach social skills or light up a couple of hundred brain cells that might languish otherwise. What parent worthy of the name will pass up an opportunity to give his kids an edge over the competition? But we talk little of the delight our children give us, both emotional and physical. Dare I say that I read to Brendan because it gives us both pleasure, a joy that is simultaneously of the immediate moment and a transmigration back to my own first moments of being read to? Much of the "useful advice" given to parents ignores the fact that it is, as often as not, our children who give us direction in how to be toward them, encouraging our behavior by exhibiting and giving pleasure.

My own earliest memory of reading is deeply physical. Funnily, it's not about my parents, who certainly did read to me and who were both great storytellers. It's of reading with another child, my best friend in nursery school. The memory dates well before I'm five, because after that he left to go to school in Swaziland and I did not see him again for twenty-five years. We are lying on the carpet of his bedroom, reading a picture book that looms in memory almost as large as ourselves. The story itself hinges on the tactile: The bunny, a piece of soft felt upon the page that one can run one's hand deliciously over, is lonely and longs for a friend. He finds an egg—cold and as hard as the rest of the cardboard—that he tries to treat as a companion until finally it cracks. Just as the rabbit is about to give in to despair, a fuzzy chick emerges from the cracked egg. I can't swear to the accuracy of this telling because I haven't read the book again since I was four. But how easily I can slip back in time to the moment my best friend and I reach forward together simultaneously as we turn to the last page and experience the tale's downy denouement with our sensitive fingertips at the same moment as we read the words aloud together.

I am connected to this moment in another way, too: in my choice of writing as a career. My first passionate involvement with literature began in my early teens—before that I had read only books about animals and was sure I would become a game ranger or naturalist—when, lonely and nostalgic in damp, cold England for the sunny land of my childhood, I picked up a collection of short stories by my friend's mother, the writer Nadine Gordimer. Her stories transported me back to the sights and sounds of the land of my exile and at the same time gave me a window into the ambivalent emotions of my adolescence. I also came to realize how individual are the books that occupy such a large place in our psyches; when I remet my childhood friend decades later in New York, he could recall nothing of the book or our reading it together.

*   *   *

So we read every night, and although the ritual stays the same, the books change according to Brendan's whim or some secret design that matches his mood. For many weeks we read *Little Babaji,* an attractively designed story about a little boy in India. The first time I read it, I was two-thirds of the way through before I recognized it as a book from my own childhood, *Little Black Sambo,* although the names have been changed and gone are the impolitic gollywog figures, replaced by authentic-looking and uncaricatured Indians. I unconsciously subvert the new version's good intentions, though, by giving each tiger an accent to distinguish him. The first tiger to appear before the proudly clad hero and tell him: "Little Babaji, I'm going to eat you up!" speaks with Winston Churchill's jowly rumble; the second is a *vairrry sinistair* Frenchman; the third a Cockney spiv; and the fourth has the swallowed consonants of Peter Sellers's comic Indian. Having once set up this pattern, I dare not deviate from it, or I will be called up short by an annoyed: "Read it properly. The funny way."

Reading aloud to my son reminds me of the possibilities of being creative as readers, to give the characters funny voices or make up things about them that aren't in the book. He is not the passive receptacle of the story but an involved listener, an equal partner in the act of reading. He constantly asks questions, makes passing commentaries, and anticipates the lines that characters are going to say. He gives the names of favorite neighbors to the three bears pictured in *Goodnight Moon* ("That's Hilary and Steven and Charlotte!"), and when these neighbors move away, he has me read that particular book over and over again so that he can nostalgically point out the resemblance. I teach literature and writing to college students, and I've found that much of my task is to encourage a return to that first dynamic engagement with books—where we can argue with them, be scared by and for the characters, thrill to their victories, and even change their fates if we want to.

Reading about the world is for Brendan as natural a way of understanding it as physically experiencing it, and he resists any attempt to separate the two into the artificial construction of the "made-up" versus the real. He is annoyed with the bullfrogs in the pond near our Vermont home; why do they not say *rrribbit* like they are supposed to? "They say *glooob*," he tells me with some disgust. Then he leans over and addresses the pop-eyed green face just visibly poking out of the water: "Come on, try to say *rrribbit!*"

Brendan often tells me he would like to be in a book, *really*. Two of his favorite books—*Cats Know Best* and *Winnie the Pooh*—show pictures of a child in the bathtub, and when we get to those pages, Brendan invariably remarks, "*I* want to be that little boy taking a bath." I suppose this is also a way of testing the limits of my parental powers, for he will ask me, "Can you put me in that story, pleeease," in the same way that he will sometimes ask me to turn him into a fish or a bird. I can remember how profoundly I, too, experienced reading as a child, sometimes being called a fibber because I would narrate events I'd read about as if they had happened to me . . . which of course they had, but not on the quotidian level. This is another gift to me that comes from reading to Brendan: to be returned to a place where one is utterly engrossed in a story, not reading to comment on it or with a mind half on something else.

Whether it is because both his parents are writers or because we read to him a lot, Brendan sees all kinds of stories as something you "read." These include occasions in the past when he was not present, such as his parents' wedding or tales of my own childhood. "Read me that story about you and Uncle Bob when you were little." These no doubt are seen as stories rather than memories because they posit the absurd notion of a time when Brendan did not exist. "Was I there, too, in Africa?" There is no satisfactory answer to the question, "Well, where *was* I before I was born?" Although he is amused by the phrase "a gleam in your daddy's eye," he clearly only lets it pass as one of those silly adult ploys to end a line of tough questioning. Memories in which he shared are clearly distinguished by his asking: "Do you remember . . ." but lately he will ask me to read him a story about the bad dream he had (featuring a ferocious dog named Lick Skunk) or about himself and Mr. Bear and how they played with keys.

Bits of what I read to Brendan reappear in surprising places. For a week or two we read *Bonjour, Mr. Satie* every night, a delightful tale involving Mr. Satie and his companion Ffortesque Ffollett who arrive at the children's house in a taxi and regale them with tales of their friends in Paris: Gertrude and Alice, and the rival painters Pablo and Henri. "Can I go to Paris sometime?" Brendan asks me, and he also wants to know what Mr. Satie is eating in the café where he runs into Picasso. "Oh, *café au lait* and croissants," I glibly reply. It is three months later, and Brendan is annoying us by his inveterate habit of climbing into the driver's seat of the car and madly turning the steering wheel. "I am driving a taxi in Paris," he tells me. "You sit in the back." So I do, and the first stop is a café. "Here is a croissant for you." He hands an imaginary object to me. "Would you like butter and jam on it? . . . Now we are driving to Gertrude's house for a delicious French meal. Rrrmm. Rrrmmm."

Although I am adamant that my reading to Brendan is not all about doing something that's good for him, I'm deeply gratified to see the way that narrative and story have become a part of the way he understands the world. I can think of nothing more important I can give him as a parent—perhaps because it's the gift my own parents gave me and one that has grown more poignant in the years since my father passed away. I was fortunate when growing up that my parents liked to tell stories and told them well, anecdotes of how they met and how they both came to be living in South Africa, where I was born. It is as if I were there when my mother at the age of sixteen took a night train out of Germany, not daring to bring any valuables with her because the border guards on the trains were notorious for their Nazi sympathies, and how in fact the train guard who was only a few years older than her was shocked almost into tears by how little money or goods she was traveling with and made sure that she would have the compartment to herself so that at least she would get some sleep. My father's anecdotes about editing a black newspaper form the fabric of my comprehension of South Africa, as strong as my own memories of the country. Good stories not only entertain us but they make us ask moral and aesthetic questions about how we conduct our lives; my father's stories of his own moments of inadvertent racism (his first day on the job he asked some black men lounging in the hallway to move the desk in his office, then apologized too many times for not recognizing them as reporters) are an indelible reminder not to get complacent about my own liberalism.

Children bring us back to our own childhoods, helping to reawaken some of the freshness of perspective that we lose in adult life. They also very palpably return us to the moments when we were children, bringing a renewed appreciation of our own parents. My father claimed that his true legacy to his grandchildren would be his nonsense songs and bad puns, and his tales of Goldberg the Rhinoceros and other African animals who resemble old Yiddish-speaking men. When Brendan delights in his own playing with words ("Mommy needs a thermometer, but you need a ther*dad*eter"), I have the uncanny feeling of being my father looking on with pride at this blond child. Then I tell some of my favorite stories from childhood—the Kalulu the Rabbit stories in *The Long Grass Whispers*—and Brendan fills in the places where I pause: "Just as Gondwa was giving the porridge to the dog he felt—" "A flick! A flick on his neck," Brendan mimes, catching me in a noose, laughing with excitement at the clever Rabbit's trickery, at the very words themselves, and I laugh at them, too, as if I'm hearing them for the first time with all my capacity for wonder intact. As I read to Brendan I feel us spinning a web of words. It is a web that was perhaps already there waiting to become visible in the light, a web that stretches both forward and back in time.

A Matter of Quality

JILL SMOLOWE

As we zoomed along I-280, just exits from home, I was beginning to feel increasingly edgy. During the course of the weekend at our country house in rural Pennsylvania, I'd had, quite literally, not so much as a minute to myself. Between the needs, demands, and wants of my four-year-old daughter, Becky, my weekend company, and my husband, I'd had no time for any of the head-clearing activities that help me renew and rearmor for the week ahead. No leisure reading. No exercise. Not even a movie video.

Now, with just a few miles and a night's sleep standing between me and the start of the new work week, I craved a few moments' silence, some time to shut down and listen to the sounds inside my own head. I turned off the CD player, which had been blasting nonstop for the last two hours, and gazed out the window. As my thoughts began to drift, I began to feel myself relax. At last some peace, some quiet, some—

"Mommy, I *said* put on 'Lucy in the Sky with Diamonds.' "

"Sweetie, we just listened to your story tape," I replied. "Remember, we take turns picking the tapes and CDs."

"But I want to hear some music," Becky said, uncharacteristically whiny after the long, hot ride.

"It's my turn to choose," I answered, resentful of her intrusion on my brief mental idyll. "I choose quiet."

"But I want to hear some music," she persisted, the whine decibels ratcheting up another notch.

"Mommy is feeling cranky," I responded irritably. "Please. Let's just be quiet for a while."

"But that's not fair. I want to hear the Beatles or—"

It was, of course, an absurd battle of wills, one that neither of us could win. As our irritation with each other mounted, I was aware that it would probably be best to put the CD on and let the mounting tension subside. But her demanding tone was fingernails on my mental blackboard. And there was something about the heat and the road that deepened my irrational obstinence. Instead of being the grown-up, I continued to go mano a mano with a four-year-old.

"We've already listened to that CD," I said testily. "It's enough."

At this point my husband interceded. "She's four years old," he murmured to me. "Knock it off."

I lapsed into a brooding silence, knowing full well that Joe was right. By the time we got home, there was just time for Becky's bath and a quick story before her bedtime. I pleaded crankiness, offered to unload the car, and pressed Joe to handle the rest. He, wisely, did not resist.

While I lugged the bags and paraphernalia into the house, I gave mental vent to my stifled frustration. *When is it my turn to read, to relax, to have some space to myself?* The anger, as usual, blew over within minutes because, in truth, I have very little to complain about on that score. By the time I ascended the stairs to give Becky her good night hug, kiss, and nightly secret (on this occasion: "Sweetheart, Mommy is very sorry she was so cranky in the car"), my irritation had been replaced by a familiar and powerful feeling of guilt.

As I unpacked the bags, I reviewed the weekend, trying to pinpoint the origin of this gust of self-reproach. Certainly, I felt no remorse for coveting some quiet time to listen to my own thoughts. How long, after all, can a forty-three-year-old woman crawl around on the floor pretending to be a puppy ("Bark, Mommy!") or feigning enthusiastic interest in a pretend tea party ("Here, eat these, Mommy!") before both mind and knees go numb?

Moreover, I came to motherhood relatively late in life, at an age when I was old enough to have a keen sense of my needs. Even as I hungered for a child, I knew that motherhood would no more answer my need to work than a child could answer my need for intimacy with my husband. As a result, I am not inclined to tear myself up wondering if Becky would be better served by my full-time attentions. Monday through Thursdays, I have a wonderful, reliable baby-sitter who deflects Becky's energy, leaving me uninterrupted blocks of time to think and write. I feel no guilt about this shared caretaking arrangement. Rightly or wrongly, I am convinced that the best mother is a happy one who feels more fulfilled than frustrated. My own sense of well-being is contingent in no small part on my work.

Perhaps, too, I've been spared the painful internal rending I see in many of my working friends because Becky, whom Joe and I adopted in China, did not enter our lives until she was seven months old. When she came into our arms for the first time, she was already a healthy, alert, loving child. Thus, from the start, it was impossible to believe that only I could meet her needs.

No, much as I would have liked to lay my discomfort on the strains of the work-child juggle, a problem that allows at least a portion of the blame to be pointed outward at an unaccommodating society, I sensed that its origin was deeply imbedded within me. It always is. That's because when it comes to Becky, my guilt is never about the time that I don't spend with her; it's about the time that I do.

As I thought more about it, I realized that my remorse stemmed from my inability to enter and exit my daughter's space on *her* time clock rather than my own. This is not new terrain for me; it's familiar territory that only frustrates more and more. Each time I feel my impatience with Becky flare, I vow anew to slow down, to build our interactions on her cues and at her pace. But I have yet to find the mechanism that can turn off my grown woman's impatience with childish things. Once it kicks in, my hunger for adult colloquy rears—be it for conversation, reading material, or simply the sound of my own thoughts—and I feel an almost uncontrollable need to bolt to my own mental space.

Too often I force the transition by inadvertently snapping in a tone that could jar, and shifting tracks with a speed that might confuse my daughter. Always, I feel guilty afterward.

Like now. Tracking back through the weekend's events, I could see how often I had demanded that her needs fall into rhythm with my own rather than the other way around. With a guest also requiring my attention, I'd carelessly responded too many times to Becky's noisy bids for attention with "Becky, please! That is *so* rude. Can't you see Mommy is talking?" I'd made the same demand in the car, expecting her one minute to accept that I'd be willing to listen to music, and the next to understand that I wouldn't. How unfair and capricious that must have seemed. How helpless she must have felt as my impatience trumped her exuberance.

Guilt, guilt. I was soaking in it an hour later as I again mounted the stairs and ducked into Becky's room for my nightly last-check ritual. I pulled up her blankets, kissed her forehead, and whispered, "Mommy loves you."

To my surprise, her eyes popped open. "Why did you say that?" she asked.

"I say it every night so you'll have sweet dreams."

"You answered my wish," she whispered.

"What was that?"

"I wanted you to come back."

Her answer, so simple, so honest, so undefended, made my heart pound. How extraordinary to be the subject of someone's most fervent wish. I hugged her a bit longer, a bit harder, knowing that the earlier irritation between us was what had kept her awake and precipitated her wish. A bit more reassurance was needed.

As I cuddled her close, I saw that we are classic co-dependents, my daughter and I. It is her unconditional acceptance of me that enables me to persist in my unacceptably snippish behavior at times. And it is my unconditional devotion to her that enables Becky to absorb my edginess and distraction without complaint. Holding her tight, I was struck anew by the power of this parenting business as I realized how grateful I was for *her* reassurance and the generosity of her forgiveness.

As One

LINDSAY FLEMING

$\mathcal{A}$ call from the school nurse came through. She had my daughter there, at her office. I might want to come and get her. Expecting a sore throat or fever, I felt uneasy when she said something about a bowel movement. She seemed reluctant to go into further detail over the phone.

Not ten minutes later I arrived at the main entrance to the Lower School, unsure where to find the nurse. Until then I'd never had occasion to speak with her or to visit her office. As soon as I opened the main door, I was met by an unmistakable odor. I moved uncertainly down the corridor, following my nose, and arrived at a door marked Health Suite. I entered. I had found the source.

The nurse sat at a desk to my left, dressed not in nurse clothes but in street clothes. She looked like a teacher or a mother—no pointed cap, no white shift. Beyond the nurse, poring over a book with another little girl, was my daughter. She had gone to school that morning in a brightly colored floral print outfit resembling cruisewear. Now she was wearing a sweatshirt and a pair of khaki pants, boy's khaki pants, too big and riding down around her hips to expose a pair of red boxer shorts with white polka dots. She appeared chipper enough, though when she saw me her expression turned contrite, sullen. She looked away and did not greet me. The nurse and I exchanged meaningful looks. A most delicate situation. Either she is afraid of punishment or she is going to punish me, I thought, as if the whole thing were somehow my fault.

I greeted them all simultaneously, brightly—"Hi!"—as if I'd been called in for a play group or a tea party. The nurse was warm, discreet, circumspect. I took my cues from her. Best not to ask. We all knew why I was there.

"I took her temperature," she said. "She doesn't have a fever." She handed me a plastic bag, knotted at the top, with a lump of soiled cruisewear inside. "You'll have to go up to the classroom and get her backpack." Of course, I said, setting the bag on the floor near her desk and turning to leave. My daughter moved to follow me. "Mommy will be right back," the nurse said. "Why don't you stay here."

I made my way down a hall festooned with colorful primary school artwork. The smell seemed to be everywhere—in the stairwell, up two floors, and already entrenched in the second grade classroom. Her teacher smiled understandingly and helped me assemble her things. Her classmates looked me over, pleased with the distraction. I scanned the faces for smirks. Nothing wayward, just curiosity. I retraced my steps to the nurse's office, the weight of complicity settling in around my heart.

"Well," I said, picking up the plastic bag. "Shall we?" We said our good-byes. The nurse asked if we'd please return the clothes; she was short, as we could see, on extras.

My daughter and I walked hand in hand down the corridor, through the front door, and into the fresh air. It was a cloudy day in late winter, with the sun now and then breaking through to wash the pavement, the dead leaves, the charcoal trees, in a more hopeful light. I decided to say nothing, to let the story emerge, if and when it did, without prodding. As we walked toward the car, I could feel her relief at leaving school, a place she loves dearly. She said nothing but broke stride to skip, just once, which seemed to me a sign that everything would be all right. I deposited the bag in the backseat, and we solemnly took our places up front. We began to drive home in mephitic silence.

It seems a good time to tell you a little bit about the heroine of this story, costumed now in boys' khakis and boxers. She is as fastidious as a cat, and rejects outfits out of hand if they look too much like boy clothes. She favors lace and velvet, anything with a sheen, sequins, hot pink, the fancier the better. She refuses to wear blue jeans. One of her favorite early books was *Going to the Potty* by Fred Rogers, with its real-life photos of children sitting on potties and a wheedling narrative about making BMs and urine (his terminology). I, on the other hand, especially disliked the book. Somehow frank treatment of the subject in the voice of Mr. Rogers fairly reeked of propaganda. Perhaps our young heroine sensed it, too, for the concept of making BM in the potty was far more exciting on the page as a pivotal plot point, a literary achievement, than it was in actual practice. Nonetheless, she asked for the book at every occasion—before bedtime and naps, and, of course, while sitting fruitlessly on her miniature throne.

Eventually she was potty trained, neither sooner nor later than the average child. Diapers were replaced by a combination of panties and Pull-Ups at bedtime. The Pull-Ups, too, were phased out in time. Potty training was not, of course, the exact end of it. I remained, not entirely by choice, closely involved in the process for a number of years, being called upon to wipe, flush the toilet, scout out restrooms in public places, and make sure the seats were suitably clean. I call this the MOM WOULD

YOU WIPE ME (MWYWM) stage after the cry that resounded at regular intervals through our home. The refrain began to run together as one whopping compound word: MOMWOULDYOUWIPEME.

How subtle the movement from MWYWM to the more stealthy, reclusive Burying stage (my own terminology). Cats, we all know, bury their waste. One of the nicest things about cats is their discretion. Our family cat, who spends a good deal of time outside the home, doesn't have a litter box. He goes to the door and meows to go out. His record is nearly impeccable. On the one occasion he smeared his reputation with an indoor accident, he had the good sense to deposit the transgression in the fireplace hearth and bury the evidence in the sand in which the gas log unit is set, the closest facsimile to a litter box he could find. He might never have been discovered had his sooty prints not betrayed him, leading away from the scene on a cream-colored rug.

Children eventually learn this burying instinct, but not until they have moved well beyond the stage of being potty trained. It happens quietly, without the fanfare of the move from diapers to MWYWM. Over time you realize that you're no longer being called to the scene to wipe up. The triumphal cry has been replaced by the telltale, if soundless, skid marks, the soiled undies. You're officially out of MWYWM. The movement has gone underground.

*   *   *

Breaking the silence a few minutes from home, she confessed in a small, wretched voice. "I went to the bathroom in my pants."

"I know, sweetie," I said in my tenderest Mr. Rogers voice. "It's okay. What happened?"

"We were in the library, and I was looking at books and I thought I had to go. I mean, I had a stomachache. It was really bad, but then it went away."

"Why didn't you ask to go?"

"Because the bathroom is so far away, and then we got our books and sat down at the table to read, and it just happened."

"And then what did you do?"

"Well, then we went to music."

*   *   *

Here we embark, as one, on our miserable odyssey. We leave the library and climb two flights of stairs to the music room, our pants smushy, our secret fetid. We feel some small relief in knowing that we are on our way to music, for the music teacher is our friend and has a loving manner; we are one of her favorites. We arrive at the music room. Perceiving a situation, the teacher tactfully asks us if we would like to visit the bathroom. Yes, we would. There we hide ourselves away in the stall, closing and bolting the door, pulling down our flashy leggings. Sadly, we realize it is too late for damage control. We have had an explosive attack of diarrhea, an accident of titanic proportions. There is no way of getting around it, cleaning it up, or otherwise masking the tragedy. We stay for a little while, squeezing our eyes tight and wishing ourselves magically home. But when we open our eyes, we are still here, in a metal box, a place we know we cannot live indefinitely. We pull up our pants, and by now the matter is smeared all up and down our legs and halfway up our backs. Our entire outfit is involved, every scrap of clothing to our socks. We wash our hands as we've been taught and muster our courage, then creep, defeated, back to face the music.

Standing in the doorway, we hope, we think, to be noticed. Our teacher interrupts Spring Sing practice to ask if we would like to go to the nurse. Yes, we'd like that very much.

*   *   *

We're home now, getting out of the car, and my daughter seems positively blithe of spirit. The cloud has lifted with her confession. I, on the other hand, am hiding a mask of pain, fully immersed in her trauma. My child went to school this morning a blank book; she has come home damaged goods, marked by a nasty entry. Will she forever be known as the girl who pooped in her pants in the library? How can we possibly face our classmates, the music room, the library ever again?

I think back to being seven, to grade two, Shelburne Elementary, Miss Pittman's class. One day while running out on the playground I got hot and stopped to peel off my sweater. My shirt came up with my sweater, exposing my flat chest. A playground teacher, some old crone whose name I do not remember, was on me in a flash; she grabbed my arm and roughly dragged me off the playground. "Don't you *ever* lift up your shirt like that." She sent me back to the classroom to contemplate my evil ways. Who did I think I was, pulling up my shirt for the boys? The shame!

The injustice! I certainly hadn't meant to flash the boys. I had no consciousness of my chest as something to be kept hidden, something that might incite trouble on the playground. She banished me from the playground in disgrace, but I knew even then that I was innocent, that it was *her* problem, not mine.

I wonder now if this accident, this incident, is *my* problem more than my daughter's. She is innocent. Why should she feel shame? Why should *I* feel shame? I imagine children to be cruel, but is it possible they might be compassionate? They might put themselves in her shoes? And what would I have done in her shoes? I would have died a slow, agonizing death in the stall. I would have waited for someone to come get me; I would not, of my own volition, have come out of the stall. Considering this, I am filled with pride for my little trouper. What courage she has; this is something in her character to celebrate. Still, my heart is knotty.

We go up to the bathroom and strip off the little boy clothes. It has been a messy affair, and although the nurse mumbled something about having cleaned her up, I'm pained afresh by the sight of her smeared, naked body. This is cleaned up? She's like a canvas crudely finger painted by some malevolent toddler. I run a hot bath with lots of bubbles. She loves baths, and today she spends a good long time in the tub while I scoop up all the soiled clothes, the cruisewear and the replacement outfit, and go to start the washing machine. Already the air has begun to clear, the smell seems finally to be gone, and my heart lifts a bit when I hear a song coming from the bathroom: "It was sa-ad when the great ship went down." Spring Sing practice has resumed.

In half an hour all traces have been washed away, the cover-up is complete. She's scrubbed clean, pink-cheeked, freshly dressed, and seated up at the counter having her favorite snack, apple slices with peanut butter. There is, in the background, the cozy sound of clothes tumbling in the dryer, the flowery scent of fabric softener in the air. We speak no more about the day but focus on the here and now: homework, half an hour of TV—oh, hell, watch as much as you want—a few games of Old Maid, make dinner, set the table. Soon Daddy is home, and when I see an opening, I fill him in privately about our ordeal. Oh, no, he says, assuming the mask of pain. Oh, yes.

We lovingly attend to her—good food, good cheer, another bath, an extra bedtime story—all the while pretending nothing is amiss. My heart is heavy. I believe her reputation will forever be tarnished by this turn of events, that she'll forever be known as the little girl who . . .

* * *

The next morning I wake her, expecting resistance and not sure how I'll deal with it. It seems important that she go to school, like getting back up on the horse. But I'm hardly prepared to play the heavy; I can't blame her if she doesn't want to go. I don't want to go either. I feel like crawling in with her, snuggling up, sailing away for a year and a day. I am guilty of over-identification. I am ashamed. No, I am the playground crone, projecting onto her my own warped worldview.

She is, however, resolute or resolved or just plain stoic. No resistance. She climbs out of bed without a moment's hesitation, and I puff briefly with pride. Such courage! Everything just as usual, I pick out her clothes (at her behest), a pretty dress, breakfast, make lunch, carpool, kiss, have a great day, and she's off, on her way toward the playground, that most vicious of childhood venues. I want to go with her as watchdog or bodyguard, to terrorize anyone who dares to poke fun. Just let them try it. I'll string them up and shove sharpened pencils . . . Impossible. I drive home, feeling strangely adrift.

In the afternoon I question her closely about the day, studying her like a zoo animal for signs of trauma. She seems fine. Unfazed. The subject never surfaces again. Buried, over, done with.

A few months later I relent to share my bed with our heroine when her father is out of town. Whenever there is a vacancy in my bed, she is eager to book passage. I discourage the practice because she is an active sleeper, a thrasher who likes to cozy up. On this night I wake to some disturbance beside me, and start to nudge her over into uncharted territory. She is talking in her sleep, though, and I lean in close, suspended over her like a Hovercraft, to make sense of a line of jumbled dialogue. One word, only one, rings clear: *library*.

She sighs deeply, tacks away from me, and falls silent on Daddy's side of the bed.

I'd like to think she's worrying over some overdue books, but a stinking, shameful tide washes over me.

I keep watch for a time, alert, scouring the horizon, ready to throw in a line. For now, the sea is calm, but I'm not fooled. Fathoms deep, the deck is being swabbed; a little sailor is hard at work.

Uprooting the Kids

FRANCINE PROSE

*W*ere anyone to ask me about the single guiltiest moment in my life as a mother so far, I could answer without hesitation. It occurred on the first night of a cross-country drive my family and I took four summers ago. We were headed for Tucson, Arizona, where I'd accepted a teaching position that required us to leave our home in upstate New York for two years. Despite a few misgivings, I was looking forward to my job. My husband, who is a sculptor, was eager to see how the Southwest might influence his work. Newborn baby Leon—two weeks old when we left New York—snoozed happily in his car seat. Only our four-year-old son, Bruno, was less than pleased.

For Bruno, the timing could hardly have been worse. Within two weeks he had lost both his place as the only child and—temporarily—his home. We had done everything we could to make these two momentous changes easier. We had spent lots of time with him during my pregnancy and explained that we would eventually be coming back; we read him picture books about the desert and about kids who had made marvelous adjustments to cross-country moves.

But something had clearly gone wrong. The first night out, we stopped at a motel by the side of the highway, somewhere near Dayton, Ohio. When we walked into the motel room, Bruno asked, "Where's the

kitchen? Where do we eat?" Then he began to cry. It soon became obvious that Bruno—unable to grasp the idea of a five-day trip—assumed we
had arrived in Tucson. In that roadside motel room, he thought he was
looking at his next two years. We assured him that this wasn't so; he said
he understood, calmed down, and then started bawling again. Perhaps he
was hungry; we hurried to a restaurant and offered him anything on the
menu. Bruno promptly lay down on the floor and, as horrified waitresses
stood by, announced, "I'm dead! I'm dead!"

It took a good six months for Bruno to adjust to his new city. And
when, in two years, we finally did return home, he spent the last fifty
miles of *that* trip singing a happy song whose only lyrics were the name of
our hometown, repeated again and again. So much for adjustment.

Many parents have experienced the guilt of dislocating a child. But
what gave my guilt a particular edge was that I wasn't—as is more com-
monly the case, I imagine—following my husband from job to job. Which
is to say I couldn't even blame the move on my husband. It was all my
fault. Forget the fact that we very much needed the job and the money—
both of which were in short supply where we had been living.

Four years after this orgy of conscience, certain details seem clearer.
There are a few things I would have done a little differently—and will do
when, this winter, we go *en famille* to Utah, where I have taken another
teaching job. This time I'll bring along photos and souvenirs of our house
and of friends and family at home—reminders for memory and for faith
that the old place and faces have not disappeared. Before leaving we'll
take even *more* time with the kids, showing them our destination on the
map, explaining how long we'll stay and what we'll do; despite our no-
table lack of success with Bruno last time, I'm still convinced that such
efforts have value.

This time I feel fairly confident that we will be easier on ourselves and on the children. One thing time and age and experience teach us, of course, is how quickly these minor troubles pass, how quickly everything passes. Realizing this gives us more flexibility, more willingness to bend. So what if we stop at every convenience store between here and the Great Salt Lake? We'll reach our destination sooner or later.

But what seems most important is that I'll stop blaming myself. Four years later, neither child seems to have been permanently scarred by our move. They're happy kids, and who knows but that living in different parts of the country may actually have done them good? And though I joke about my absolute worst fantasy—grown-up Bruno has committed some terrible crime, and a TV announcer solemnly intones, "His parents moved around a lot"—it seems unlikely.

In retrospect, and without the distorting lens of guilt, things seem clearer. Bruno's dramatic reaction of playing dead on the restaurant floor was not simply an expression of acute pain but also a reflection of the fact that he is—and always has been—a theatrical child. And that couple grimly driving the interstate—heading for the desert with a newborn and an unhappy four-year-old—don't seem like terrible parents at all but, rather, like admirably brave ones.

I still worry about uprooting the children, pulling them from their comfortable home and schools for a sojourn into the unknown. What comforts me is having seen the passage of time turn extremes of past guilt into almost funny family history. And what reassures me most is this: When Bruno was recently asked by his second-grade teacher to draw his favorite landscape, he drew a bright and sunny and glorious desert scene.

Of Names and Hair

VALERIE WILSON WESLEY

I came of age during the civil rights movement of the 1960s with a strong sense of racial identity. I knew I would give my children African names. Call it a way to connect to the Motherland or the simple need to play out my generation's rage, but I didn't want any Helens, Beckys, or Dannys in my family. Giving your child a "slave name," which was what we called names of European origin in those days, was tantamount to teaching her that light skin was more desirable than dark.

Although I was too young to have fought the early battles for racial justice—I never had my head bashed in at a Woolworth's lunch counter in Georgia or risked my life riding a Greyhound bus south—I understood the meaning of segregation. The memory of Emmett Till, the young Chicago boy who went south for the summer and was lynched for whistling at a white woman, weighed heavily on the minds of all black parents, and I was warned about the ways of southern whites. I was told by my grandmother to run in the opposite direction if a white man so much as nodded in my direction. She understood the vulnerability of black women and that if a young black girl was raped or assaulted by a white man, her word against his didn't count for spit. I was also cautioned never to venture into white neighborhoods—not even in the light of day.

Although I attended a predominantly white school in the Connecticut town where I grew up, I never felt as if I really belonged. I did have best friends, although they seemed to disappear when I reached adolescence, and I got along fine with the boys in my class until it was time to choose a square dance partner. The only African-American hero I learned about was George Washington Carver, who did some unusual things, albeit important, with a peanut.

So when I had kids, I was determined that they would not only be steeped in African-American history but would understand their worth as black women. Part of that sense of worth, I believed, would come from names that connected them to their ancestral past—before slavery and segregation. The other part would come from loving and accepting who they were, which meant never straightening their hair. The names I settled on—Thembi, for my oldest daughter, and Nandi, for my youngest—were traditional Zulu names offered by a friend, a visiting professor from South Africa who was active in the fight for freedom. I liked the way these names rolled off my tongue, and they seemed to suit my daughters. I braided my girls' hair in tight, elaborate cornrows, and when Nandi begged "to look more like Mommy," I bought her a pair of gold earrings like mine and proudly cut her hair into a cute Afro.

Although my girls seemed to love their names when they were small, something happened when they reached eight and five. Thembi became Tiffany, and Nandi became Amber. They also developed a fondness for covering their hair with towels and swinging their tresses around like Farrah Fawcett in *Charlie's Angels.*

I was devastated. Despite all the books I had bought with black characters and our discussions about African and African-American history, my daughters seemed to be rejecting their names and their God-given hair. Would they grow up wanting to be white? We lived in a well-integrated town, but my kids were the only black children on our street. I had known black people reared in all-white environments who never seemed to come into their own. They were uncomfortable in their skin—more white than black. They had only whites as friends and seemed ill at ease with other black people. They shunned African, African-American, and Caribbean culture, and worshiped any and everything that came from Europe. We called them Uncle Toms in the sixties. They were considered sell-outs. Oreos. I certainly didn't want my daughters growing up to be like them. Where had I gone wrong? I wondered. Had I emphasized black culture to the point where they were rejecting it?

When I asked my daughters about their name changes, they were matter-of-fact. "They are our play names," my youngest daughter reassured me.

"But nobody else has play names."

"Nobody else has names that sound like ours."

"What about those towels on your heads?"

"Play hair," my oldest daughter, Thembi, said with a shrug. My youngest daughter, whose little Afro was always complimented by my politically aware friends, nodded in agreement.

Yet their "play" seemed a rejection of everything I stood for, so I was still worried. But I knew the danger of ignoring a child's feelings and bending her to your will. I had a graduate degree in early childhood education and considered myself an enlightened parent. I had never been comfortable with authoritarianism, and I had always challenged and fought the system. Outside of gently discussing their choices with my kids, I wasn't sure what I should do.

An African-American parent can't afford to forget that race makes a difference in America, or her children will pay the price. To teach a child otherwise is to teach her a lie that will leave her vulnerable. There will always be the child who is uncomfortable in her presence, the teacher who has low expectations, the store detective who assumes she will steal. And when a child confronts racism, she has to know where to put it. She has to understand that the problem lies not with her but with the racist, and that although it's fine to be angry, she can't be consumed by rage.

But a child is a child, and there is a thin line between teaching her the truth about American racism and encouraging her to become obsessed by it. It's a balancing act that all black parents have to learn. You never know if you have done too much or too little. You also bring your own racial baggage—which we all carry if we grow up in America, no matter what color we are—and those heavy bags can be hard to put down.

So I bought more books, took them to more cultural events, and tried to make sure that the negative images of African-Americans that so often filled the television screens didn't do any permanent damage. We continued to celebrate Kwanzaa with friends, and my daughters knew more African-American history than a lot of adults I knew. Nevertheless, a couple of years later Thembi—who *never* wanted to look "more like my mommy"—announced that she was straightening her hair. Play names and towels were one thing; straightening her hair was another matter altogether.

I had always had deep feelings about hair. When I went off to Howard University in 1965, I wore a wig. I didn't think anything about it. Nearly everybody I knew wore one. I thought mine made me look like Mary Wilson of the Supremes. But by the end of my freshman year the political climate of black America had changed. I snatched off my wig, stopped straightening my hair, and cut it close to my scalp in a short natural hairdo that was chic and *very* radical. It was a declaration of independence.

My parents, their friends, and even some of the proper folks who saw me on the street were horrified. Middle-class black girls did not go *au naturel*. A hairstyle was a socioeconomic statement, and *proper* black women looked, spoke, and dressed a certain way. They didn't rock the boat. They tried to make the white folks comfortable, and one did that by looking as "white" as possible. The straighter hair was, the better it was—be it natural or achieved with a hot comb or lye, quaintly called "hair relaxer." Black women, no matter what age, wore a wig or permed the life out of their hair. It was a mark of womanhood. You got your period and you straightened your hair.

When I stopped straightening mine, I felt as if I had reclaimed some forgotten or lost part of myself. (An added bonus was that all the serious young political men on Howard's campus loved it—which is as important as politics when you're nineteen years old. We weren't feminists yet.) My hair was a rejection of the old definitions of beauty. It was saying, I am who I am, and I am proud of that, and that I would be completely and irrepressibly myself.

In my youth, a free mind and "fried" hair just weren't considered compatible. So Thembi's declaration of independence—quickly followed by Nandi's—surprised and alarmed me.

My first reaction was to forbid it.

"No way will you use chemical straighteners!" I said.

"You can't tell me what to with my own hair!" Thembi responded.

"Same for me," Nandi tossed in. (They have always challenged me as a team.)

"It is *our* hair," Thembi added.

"They have a point," my husband agreed. (He has always been a wimp when it comes to our daughters.)

I realized then that I was defeated. I didn't "officially" give my permission but rather slunk out of the room and back into the memories of my youth and my own rebellious step into womanhood. Next thing I knew, they were both sporting flips. Sullenly, I accepted it.

And maybe that was where my objections belonged. In many ways the world I had known as a girl was vastly different from the one my daughters were growing up in. Racism was still as insidious as ever, but it was far more covert and indirect, and the battles my daughters would wage would not be the same as mine. Their weapons would be different. Their strategies would be new ones. The battleground had changed. I had fought the great hair and name fight, so maybe now they were at last free to call themselves what they wanted and wear their hair any way they wanted. It was one less barrier to break down.

My daughters are women now. Nandi is twenty-three, and Thembi is twenty-six. They are sure of themselves and their identity. They have faced down blatant and subtle racism and come out stronger for the encounter. They are tough, independent women—sure of themselves, proud of their history, but firmly planted in the here and now. They are becoming the kind of women I enjoy talking to and spending time with. They both wear their hair natural—no wigs, chemicals, or towels—and they tell me they will definitely give their children African names. I recently asked Nandi what things I had done during their childhood that most gave them a strong sense of identity. Was it the books? The censoring of negative stereotypes? Their names?

"Everything you did and said was important. Mainly we watched how you dealt with racism and learned from that. Those were the important lessons," Nandi said, and then added, "But when I was four, why did you make me wear that Afro? I was the only kid in the whole damn school who had one. I still meet people who remember it!"

I can't say that I was surprised. What I thought was right for Nandi at four was not by the time she was ten, and she told me so. I had taught my girls to make decisions, and they were eager to make them—on their own. If you encourage your daughters to find themselves, they usually end up becoming just who you hope they will be. Mine did in the end—with their names and, finally, their hair intact.

Soccer Practice

KEVIN CANTY

This was a few years ago in the South. We were newly transplanted there, my wife and I and our small children, and new to prosperity. I had just started to teach writing at a college, my first real job. We had a plain brick house on a fancy street, a Volvo station wagon, and a retirement plan.

I felt like a complete fake, of course, and kept waiting for the fraud police to come and make us give it all back. For almost a decade we had been living like fugitives, moving from state to state, through graduate school and the beginnings of a writing career. Even before that, my wife and I had run with musicians, artists, photographers. We were related to people who had real jobs, but none of our friends did.

Now we were trying to switch sides. I got a haircut and bought some brown shoes to wear to work. Still the lives of our neighbors—straight white Christian Republicans for the most part—remained as mysterious as ever behind their azalea hedges and the hum of the air conditioners. Looking back, I can see that we were lost, neither one thing nor the other. But we didn't know it at the time.

The second spring we were there, we volunteered our first-grade son for a soccer league. It was a choice that went along with our new station in life; it seemed like the kind of thing we ought to do. It didn't feel like us, the people we had been, but there were so many new things in our lives, things to get used to. It couldn't hurt.

Besides, Turner was (and is) a friendly, smart, and agile child, capable of physical feats. He could hike all afternoon without complaint, ski cross-country, shoot a basketball. But he was a quiet boy. In the six years since he had been born, we had lived in five houses: one in Florida, two in Arizona, a log cabin in Montana, and now this new place in North Carolina. All this moving around had left him a little shy, a little inward, slow to adjust to this new circumstance and a little suspicious of it. He wasn't unhappy, I don't think, although I'm never sure of my children's happiness. He was just quiet and turned in toward himself, the kind of boy who could spend two hours drawing picture after picture of a diplodocus until he got it right.

Soccer, then, would be good for him, good for all of us. It would bring him out. It would help us all fit in. This was the plan.

Everything went fine at first. We got him shin guards and real soccer shoes, which pleased him very much. Lucy, my wife, was the one who took him to practice at first, and she reported that everybody was very nice and that Turner was enjoying himself. Even in the beginning she seemed a little skeptical; this wasn't quite our kind of thing. It felt like trying on a suit of somebody else's clothes. But we were both willing to give it a try.

I picked him up from practice a couple of times, and it seemed okay—an idyllic little scene, in fact, the late-afternoon sun slanting through the tall trees that ringed the field, the green grass, the kids in uniforms taking turns at some elaborate kicking drill. The coach, a volunteer, was young and friendly and no Nazi; his assistant coach was his fiancée, who I remember mostly as a head of sparkly blond hair and a pair of long, athletic, deeply tanned legs. They were friendly, and Turner was doing about as well as any of the other boys. I was proud of him. Everything was fine.

Practice turned to games, though, and when Lucy brought him back from the first one, she was bothered. She couldn't quite say what the problem was, and I didn't think too much of it. Some little difficulty of adjustment. But when she came back from the second one, she was still disturbed by something. She said, "He's not quite getting it."

"Give him time," I said. "It's only his second game."

"I don't know. You should come and see him."

"I will," I said—and then I didn't, not until a few more games into the season. There was the usual array of excuses large and small: I was working, doing errands, flying around with my landlord in his antique single-engine plane. Then Lucy's job switched around so she was working weekends. Then it was my turn, for the rest of the season, to go to the games.

This was springtime, Saturday mornings at ten-thirty or eleven. The weather was beautiful every day that I remember. The light was low and soft and yellow, and the dew was still on the grass. I felt the optimism and expectancy that I get when I look at an empty baseball stadium. Not that this was empty. There was an early game and a late game, and the playing fields, alive with running boys and girls in uniform, were lined with yelling parents. We had to hunt for a place to park among the Lexuses and Range Rovers and Explorers. Despite living only eight or ten blocks from the YMCA, we were a little late. We were always a little late.

In a rush, then, with his hair uncombed and his shin guards crooked, I sent Turner off to join the team while I collected his sister, Nora, and the several small things a two-year-old needs: juice, blanket, friendly toys. I had not showered myself, having been writing until ten minutes before game time. I arrived on the sideline feeling straight out of Ellis Island, dirty and disorganized and laden with bundles. This was not the case with the other parents. They looked like models out of the Sunday paper, the women in skorts and lavender tops and the husbands dressed in Polo and Ralph Lauren, smelling of cologne in the cool morning air. They were madly friendly, at least at first, but there was no getting around the fact that I did not look like them.

Then the game began.

Turner didn't play at first, which bothered me more than it did him. The boys and girls raced back and forth, a little knot of colored ants at the far goal, then following the ball past us and gaining faces—sweaty, intent little faces—and then past us and gone again. Turner, I noticed, was making something out of blades of grass instead of following the game. His team scored, and all his teammates leaped and cheered, everybody but Turner. He didn't seem to notice at all. He was concentrating on the thing he was making.

Then it was his turn to play, and I saw what Lucy was talking about. He ran out onto the field, the whistle blew, and he ran with the pack, chasing down the ball. Turner was keeping up and running and looking like all the rest except that he wouldn't pay attention. The ball would slip right past him. Once he nearly tripped over it; a few minutes later he ran right past it. A plain black-on-white soccer ball sitting dead in the grass not five feet in front of him, and he ran right past it, leaving it wide open for the opposing team, who promptly scored against us.

Worse: As I watched him running with the others, I noticed that he would sometimes dart off to the side to take a shot at an imaginary ball, as if rehearsing. He would stop short unexpectedly or keep running right through the whistle. At first I wondered if he was feeling well, but he seemed fine; he seemed like himself.

After ten or fifteen minutes, I figured out what was going on: While the nineteen other children were playing an actual game of soccer out there on the actual field, my son was playing an imaginary game of soccer in his head. The fact that he was running up and down the field in their company was mere coincidence. The others were actually playing soccer, but Turner was just pretending to.

I was not the only one to notice either. A zone of silence grew around Nora and me as the other parents edged away, intently cheering their own sons and daughters on while politely trying not to notice that my son was screwing up the game for everybody. The fiction is that these games are not competitive, that the kids are there to learn important lessons in teamwork and cooperative play; but nobody who has spent five minutes on the sidelines of a game will believe this. In fact, the parents whip themselves up into a white-hot frenzy of competitiveness, hoping and cheering not only that we beat the other team but that their own Corey or Darla or Turner would be the one to score the crucial goal. And I can't leave myself out of this. I can only assume that if Turner were the leader of the pack, the red-faced demon swooping down on his opponents, I would have yelled as loud and as long as any of the rest of them.

He wasn't, though. He dallied and dreamed, and after a while the coach took him out, to the relief of everybody.

Everybody but Turner, I mean. This whole episode was sliding right by him. He never gave a sign that he noticed anything was amiss; he continued to build things out of grass while the game was in progress, chatted with his friends—he had a couple of friends on the team—and looked forward to the snacks.

I, on the other hand, was in agony. The other parents stood and cheered, and none of them would look at me. "Go, Corey!" yelled one set of parents. "Go, Corey! Go, Corey!" Corey was big and strong and Most Likely to Succeed and scored about half the goals for our side, and his name burned in my ears. When Turner was in the game, I yelled out things like "Pay attention!" and "The ball's over there! Where's the ball, Turner?"

He looked at me sometimes, confused. There was an edge to my voice that he wasn't used to, that he wasn't expecting. Besides, I was interrupting his daydream. I tried to hide my anger and embarrassment, but they sometimes crept out. By the time we made it home that day, I was exhausted from these waves of feeling.

The next Saturday, Turner was no different. I was worse. Partway through the game, I took Nora on an extended walk around the soccer fields, just so I wouldn't have to watch. But the game seemed to follow me—"Go, Corey! Go, Corey!"—and I could not forget. There were five other games in progress, and in none of them did I see any child acting as foolishly and aimlessly as my son. I went back and stood alone on the sidelines, a careful few feet from the other parents, and I watched Turner making things out of the grass between his feet and I burned inside.

Never mind that this is the only personality he's got.

Never mind that this is the person I love.

Never mind that this same dreamy concentration is the thing that enables him to build huge constructions and castles out of kid junk and assorted toys, that lets him draw beautifully and memorize the known facts about reptiles, that combines intelligence and focus and creativity in a way that will make him capable of great things later. Never mind that I was embarrassed about the best parts of his mind.

Never mind that this is the same exact way I was at his age, that I was never one of the scorers or one of the leaders or one of the little tow-headed conquerors. No, I was the solitary, the kid who would go out to the track in the early morning and run by myself, the one who swam a mile every day in the thirty-foot pool, two hundred lengths.

Never mind that these same clean Americans in plaid shorts and cologne had never let me in the club, were not about to let me into the club now, no matter what my son did or didn't do.

No, I wanted impossible things from my son. I wanted him to be socially easy, physically gifted, a mover and a mixer, all the things I have never been—at the same time never losing his intelligence or his focus. I wanted him to be the child he was, the child I loved, and at the same time I wanted him to be one of the little conquerors. And at that time I could not see the things he was, the things I loved. I could only hear the other parents in my ears—"Go, Corey!"—and feel the blood rushing to my face as he dawdled and dreamed his way across the field. I was embarrassed because he was the child he has always been. I was angry with him for not living up to the expectations of these strangers. I walked away from the field as if he were not my child.

That is what I mean when I say we were lost.

PART III

TAKING WING

Childtime

NOELLE OXENHANDLER

"What did you today?" my husband asked me one evening when I was sitting at the dinner table, stuck and silent, like a pillar of salt.

"Nothing," I said. It had been one of those days that dissolves in a whir of unsuccessful errands, unreturned phone calls, malfunctioning machinery, piles of junk mail.

But Ariel, who was six at the time, looked at me across the table.

"That's not true!" she said, and there was genuine distress in her voice, as if she had caught me out in a big lie. "You did a lot today."

"Like what?" I asked, surprising myself at how much I suddenly needed to hear her answer.

"You mixed that color of blue paint that I wanted for my clay necklace. You crawled under my bed and found that black shoe I'd been looking for. And you went to the store and bought four tapioca puddings."

That moment for me was a bit like the famous duck-rabbit drawing when suddenly, in a kind of shimmer, the outline you've been staring at transforms into a completely different shape. Through Ariel's eyes I glimpsed the possibility that my day had been sufficient unto itself and my existence quite justified.

Without hesitating, she had reeled my day's achievements off like a list, yet it was a list that had utterly nothing to do with the one I had made for myself that morning, with its unrelenting mix of writerly and household tasks. Her response made me aware that normally I look at myself and what I've accomplished through such a narrowly focused lens that when I tally up at the end of the day, much of what I do doesn't even make it on my list. *Finish book review / workshop calls / cat medicine* might appear on my list, but *the color blue?* Never.

Of course, I realized that Ariel's lens was rather narrowly focused, too, revolving as it did around her own small-girl needs and desires. And while it seemed to me unlikely that I might ever see the purchase of four tapioca puddings as the lion's share of a day well spent, still, there was something about her list that came through like a signal. It came through like the sound of a small bell in fog or like Hansel's white pebbles making a path in the dark. And for a while in the wake of that conversation, whenever I felt myself begin to wither in my own harsh glare, I would try to bask in Ariel's more forgiving gaze.

It was hard, harder than I had expected, for I was not only up against my own deeply ingrained habits but against the very grain of the culture we live in. Isn't the sense of time as pressure a virtual constant of contemporary life? I know that I tend to experience time as both the measure and the medium of my existence—a measure against which I constantly fall short because as medium there is simply never enough, never enough. It is as though I were trapped in a small chamber in which, although there was never enough oxygen, my sense of self-worth depended on being able to fully extend my lungs. Isn't this the definition of a double bind? *You can't and you must. You must and you can't.*

And then one afternoon, as I was looking through an album of photographs from my own childhood, I felt the duck-rabbit shimmer again— only this time from the opposite point of departure. I had come across the scenes of a camping trip to Maine that my parents and I had taken when I was five. There, in faded black and white, were the birch trees sending their dappled light over the water and rocks, and so much came back to me. I remembered the birch bark tepee and canoe that my father had made for my Iroquois doll, with her black braids and deerskin dress. I remembered the penny he had placed on the railroad track just before a train came and that, in a moment's whoosh, was magically made flat for me. And I remembered my mother comforting me when I saw a small green frog swallowed by a black snake and the celebration chant she sang with me when, the very next day, I saw the same green frog—only now he was black—come alive again. It went something like this:

> *Green frog, green frog, where did you go?*
> *Into the snake's belly, black, black—*
> *And now we are glad, we are glad*
> *You've come back!*

I floated for a while in these memories, and then I tried an odd experiment: switching the lens. With what I know now about my parents' lives at that time, I realized that in the very midst of this camping trip, my father was probably obsessing about his unfinished Ph.D. thesis and my mother was anxious about my father's obsession as well as her own unpainted paintings and our unfurnished apartment back in the city.

Who can say whose take on that time was the true one? The projects my parents were fretting about have long since surrendered their urgency, but those moments we spent in Maine have remained among the most powerful of my childhood memories. They were formative moments, too, in ways that my parents couldn't have known at the time.

There was something about the transformations I witnessed—the pink-white piece of birch bark folding into tepee and canoe; the penny, in an instant, spread paper-thin and oblong under the train's whir and clatter—that gave me a sense I have never lost of the liquid nature of things, the way that even something hard or dry can overflow its boundaries, spill into a different shape. And although years later I realized that the black frog couldn't possibly have been the same green frog who had been swallowed, still—absurd as it may seem—that early experience is inextricably linked for me with a deep sense of hope in the way life renews itself that I have never completely lost.

*　　*　　*

If we are, in a poet's phrase, "small gods" to our children, they are, in their own way, small gods to us. Although in their immense need of attention they devour our time, they also lavish upon us their own brand of infinity, the infinity of the unhurried present moment. Although they multiply exponentially the number of errands and obligations on our lists, at the same time they release us from that list. They redeem us from the oppressive sense of time as pressure and measure by opening us to a very different dimension.

Stooping to water a plant or dead-head a flower on my way to do a dozen More Important Things, I might suddenly find myself absorbed in a world of ants who are traveling along stems and leaves as if they were a vast arterial network of highways and rest stops. Such moments happened frequently when my daughter was small, without my even trying. "Mom, come look at the beautiful fly!" my neighbor's four-year-old son called out to her the other day. "How could a fly be beautiful?" she thought to herself. But when she went to have a look, he told her, "See the rainbows in its wings?"

Some time ago a friend told me about her graduation that followed a prolonged course of medical training. Along with rigorous academic work, the program had involved the exhaustion and turmoil of many sleepless nights and a constantly changing schedule of clinic duty. She felt such enormous relief at having come through the ordeal that, in the midst of all the balloons and champagne at the celebration party, she found herself repeating, like a mantra, the word "never": *I'll never have to write another paper. I'll never have to take another exam. . . .* "I thought I was just saying the words to myself," she told me. But her seven-year-old daughter overheard her and said, in a stricken voice, "Mama, do you mean you're never going to play school anymore?" For a moment, my friend told me, she almost wished she could go back and write one more paper, take one more exam, just to see how different it all might have been if she had been able to approach it as "playing school."

*   *   *

If there is something divine, there is also a kind of trickster or court-fool energy about our children when they are young. They impede us, thwart us, pull the rug out from under our serious selves—but in so doing they gift us, grace us, surprise us.

Not long ago a friend told me about just such an incident that occurred a few years ago, in the midst of one of the most stressful periods of her life. The mother of three young children, she was going through a difficult divorce while holding down a very demanding job at a large hospital. On this particular evening she had an important report due the next day, and feeling overwhelmed with it all, she decided to save time by taking the three children out for a quick bite of dinner before returning to finish her work at home. The children took the last bite of their desserts, and Dana was just getting ready to pay the bill and leave when the children discovered the elaborate "Customer Survey" forms that were stacked under the salt and pepper shakers. With painstaking conscientiousness, they began to fill out the forms. Then the questions began: "Mom, what does 'prompt' mean? " "What's a 'garnish?' "

"You know that painting *The Scream?*" Dana asked me while recounting this story. "That's how I felt. That scream was rising inside me. I bit my lip and thought I might implode right there in that little vinyl booth. And then I started to laugh. It was just so absurd. We sat there for twenty minutes, carefully writing and erasing and writing again with our number two pencils."

Although my own daughter is twelve now and her own trickster self is increasingly hostage, alas, to the self-consciousness of early adolescence, she still possesses an uncanny ability to throw me off-course. The other night I had one of those dreams about being late for everything and bringing all the wrong papers. In the morning I woke feeling both groggy and so tight with anxiety that I could barely turn my head. I came staggering into the kitchen to make myself a cup of coffee, for which I felt more desperate than usual. But Ariel, who was already up and fully launched on her day, followed me into the kitchen and said, "Wait."

"What?" I said, and it came out in a snarl.

"I want to put this tattoo on you," she said. She made me stand there a full minute, absorbing the odor of mildew, as she pressed a paper tattoo with a damp sponge next to my right eye. It felt like an incredibly long

minute, and like my friend Dana in the restaurant, I found myself wanting
to scream.

But I didn't. And for the rest of the day, whenever I glanced in the
mirror, I was surprised to see a small blue squirrel at the edge of my eye.
All day long I resisted the impulse to wash it off. After all, I reminded myself, soon she'll be caught in the same time vise as I, and then where I will
turn for those moments of utterly unexpected release from my own
agenda?

*   *   *

A beautiful fly. Playing at school. A blue squirrel next to my eye.
Aren't these the reasons we wanted children in the first place, to mix up
our categories, to rearrange the rigid shapes of our lives, to take our
ducks in a row and, in a sudden shimmer, make them turn into rabbits
and back again? If I hadn't been there with my father in Maine, would he
have found the time to bend a piece of birch bark into tepee and canoe
shapes? I never thought of it that way before—all the time I gave him.
Every day when he came home from work, I would make him stand in
the doorway while I searched the cuffs of his pants for hidden treasures
among the bits of lint and dust: a coin perhaps, a paper clip. Was it a long
minute for him, standing there, as it was for me in the kitchen the other
day receiving my blue tattoo? What a gift!

One day when Ariel was three and I was at my desk working hard on
a book, she sat on the floor at my feet in deep concentration. One by one
she removed the long punched-hole edges of computer paper that I had
thrown in the wastebasket, and one by one she stuffed them into a red

sock. It was a large red sock, and it took her small hands a long time to stuff it. Since that time we've moved across the country and lived in three different houses. I've had to let go of hundreds of objects, but I've never been able to part with that sock. Now I feel closer to understanding why. I look back at that scene, and this is what I see: a mother, frantic with deadline—because it's hard to write a book and even harder when you're the mother of a small child who devours your time—sits hunched at her desk. At her feet, her daughter sits, linking her mother to another world. In this world there are no deadlines. Work is play, and there is all the time in the universe to do what one is doing, to have done what one has done. In this world an orphaned red sock is filled to overflowing with what a mother has cast out. A green frog leaps into life again, black. And "You mixed the color blue" can be a fitting epitaph—not just for a day but for a life.

$\mathcal{L}ooking\ \mathcal{A}way$

CAROL MUSKE-DUKES

$\mathcal{I}$t was bedtime for my five-year-old daughter, Annie. It was a cool spring night, and Annie's father was out of town. An actor, he spent many days on location or onstage far away—and Annie had decided (as she often did) to camp out in my bed. She loved settling in with her stuffed animals (a fox and a dazed-looking dog-eared dog), listening to stories, and then drifting off to sleep next to me.

The rituals of bedtime were soothing to both of us. After a warm bath, fresh pajamas, maybe some hot chocolate, she'd settle in bed, and I would read her a story or two, *The Big Orange Splot* or *Where the Wild Things Are.* Then perhaps I'd launch into one of my own haphazard and meandering narratives, such as "Henry, Girl of the North" or the adventures of Toobie Bandolatz, a souped-up surfboard.

On this particular night I was distracted. I read the story, whatever it was, a bit hastily. We said prayers, speeding through the "God blesses," rattling off names of relatives and friends: quick pats on invisible heads. Then I switched off the bedside lamp and readied myself for the ten minutes or so it would take my child to begin breathing deeply, rhythmically. This was a time, for me, of astonishing sweetness, coupled with fierce self-vigilance. As an overworked (often "single") mother, teacher, and writer, I had to guard against a deeply pleasurable instinct: floating off to sleep, breathing in tandem with my little girl. Sometimes I shook myself out of a steep vertical plunge into unconsciousness, startling awake, gasping.

What was keeping me from falling peacefully asleep beside my child? All day long I worked hard at teaching and parenting. Didn't I deserve to rest? Didn't my daughter deserve to have her mother relaxed and breathing safely beside her?

Well, yes, yes to everything. But the fact was, and is, that I reserved the hours after Annie went to sleep for my own work. (That is, after I washed the dinner dishes, walked the dogs, returned phone calls, made Annie's lunch for kindergarten the next day, and so forth.) There were my writing projects: a cluster of poems, a novel, a critical essay, an op-ed piece. I prided myself on this ability of mine to start my own work late at night—sometimes after 10 P.M. Often I would work until two in the morning, swept up on a current of solitary, uninterrupted composition—no phones ringing; no doorbells, handymen, postmen; no expectations beyond what my imagination asked of me. And it asked a lot. Out of my exhausted mind, pages of writing unscrolled. I sped from poetry to fiction to criticism.

I felt my daughter relaxing beside me. Through the second-floor bedroom windows floated the Los Angeles night. The sky had darkened from the pink and violet of early evening, yet somehow retained its paleness. Now and then a soundless, lit plane far away seemed to move in tiny increments—just beyond the tops of houses and the streaks of cloud, just beyond the dark hedge, its steady exhalation of the heady scents of night-blooming jasmine and honeysuckle. The moon slowly rose.

Suddenly there was a bright loud chirping noise. A mother bird (a swallow, I think) had made a nest for her offspring in the top of the cypress tree outside the window. The nestlings peeped a little, sleepily, then the mother bird spoke to them and they quieted.

"Annie," I whispered, eager not to miss this opportunity for extending the empire of maternal love, "listen to that. That mama bird is saying good night to her little ones. Just like us." I couldn't stop myself: "I'll bet she's saying prayers with them."

Annie turned her head slowly on the pillow to face me. Her eyes were half-lidded, her voice dreamy and slow.

"Yes," she whispered back, "but that mama bird is not going to get up in a little while and write a novel."

Well, how cute *and* utterly devastating—one of those cautionary tales about how children come to understand power. I laughed; she did not. She was sleeping. I stayed up the rest of the night, lying rigid beside her, interrogating myself. The mother bird had a few more comforting words to say to her young, there beyond the window, but she had no comforting words for me. She knew I had a novel to write.

Annie was conceived when I was thirty-six years old and pretty clear about what I wanted from life. I had published books, I taught poetry and fiction. I also had been fairly certain that I did not want children. I had seen my own mother give up so much. She had wanted to be a writer; her six children had ensured that her energies would go places other than the waiting page. In August 1981 I went to Italy on a Guggenheim Foundation fellowship for poetry. I rented an airy top floor above an inner courtyard with a fountain and a wall built by the Etruscans; overlooking the blue vineyard valleys outside Florence, it was in a little town called Barbarino Val d'Elsa. A professor friend (I was teaching then in the graduate writing program at Columbia) and his wife had rented a house just down the winding cobbled street. I sat in a red wooden chair at my desk, looking out the windows at the hills over the stone wall of my high terrace, writing—putting together poems for a new book. Every night I had a perfect Tuscan dinner at one of the little restaurants nearby with my friends. Sometimes we walked up the dusty roads to local vineyards and bought wine poured into green glass bottles from the storage vats. Then one day my friend, the poet Jorie Graham, invited me to her parents' extraordinary house (a renovated twelfth-century church) in Todi, Perugia. She suggested I drive down with an actor friend of her brother's. The plan was that I meet him in Florence, then ride with him to Todi. His name was David Dukes, and he was shooting a TV miniseries called *Winds of War* in Florence with Ali MacGraw, Robert Mitchum, and many other American actors.

I cared about none of this. I had so little interest in actors and acting that I prayed I would not have to talk much on the ride out of Florence. Anyway, to condense the story (which begins to sound suspiciously like a fairy tale), I met David and we fell in love and later married. Our courtship is not the subject of this essay, but there is one significant fact attached to our meeting in terms of the parenting question: Jorie had not told me that David was a father. His adolescent son, Shawn, skinny, gangly, and awkward, was with him. He followed David everywhere like a duckling. I gradually learned the history of David's marriage at nineteen to a young woman from New Zealand whose family had been traveling through San Francisco, where David's family lived. They dated, she got pregnant, there was a wedding, and not that long after, a divorce. The mother kept Shawn with her on her travels for a while, then sent him winging to David in California.

I had been married and was now divorced myself; the separation had been amicable, but there were no children, for which I was thankful. I had come to believe that most people my age just hadn't grown up enough, even in their thirties, to know how to handle kids. Now I witnessed a man who casually included his son everywhere he went, who taught him manners, who asked his opinion most of the time. I was impressed. Later I discovered that David felt guilty about his "inadequacies" as a parent. His peripatetic acting career had forced him to place Shawn in a boarding school. David did spend most of the summer months with Shawn—flying him to wherever he was working or bringing him home to the house he owned in L.A. It was not round-the-clock fatherhood, but this did not change my impression that I was dealing with a person who was a true adult. And adulthood had become connected, in my mind, with being a parent.

For the first time I began to believe that having a child might not be an endeavor doomed to failure or conflict, although this thought did not consciously enter my mind at that lovely juncture of two lives in Italy. At that point I recorded glimpses of my new friend straightening his son's collar, pointing out a scene from a guidebook, offering him a pale green gelato in a thick soft cone. I believed that I was learning something new about love.

Now I was again learning something new about love—and guilt. David's guilt made him fear the idea of a second child, and he had gone warily into parenthood with me. Oddly, I'd taken the lead. I, of all people, felt confident about being a parent. I thought I could continue to write and teach and be a good mother. I would find a way to manage it all.

What I did not want to be was the kind of mother who *looked away*. A poet friend had told me that her earliest memories of her mother (a well-known artist) were of her mother's face turned away, staring off into middle distance, preoccupied by work, thinking. I did not want to be that turned-away face. I did not want to be preoccupied when my daughter looked at me.

And now, despite all my careful attention, my daughter had caught me out. She had picked up on my nervous anticipation and my need to hurry; she had picked up on my late-night obsessions.

Had I thought that these two elements would not leak, blending into each other? Why had I made the assumption that my daughter would not notice that I was often writing in my head while I talked to her? Did I think she wouldn't catch me looking away?

*   *   *

It took me a while to realize that I was not the mother bird. I was not about to spend my whole life sitting in my nest. I'd provide the "nest" and all that went with it, but I also had to devote the time I needed to my own work. I was going to try my best to be "present" for her every moment that I was with her, but I would fail. I would fail time and time again, and I would continue to feel guilty.

This was an important revelation for me: that guilt is ongoing, that it attends every emotional situation, that it punctuates love and hate and loss—and the sense of failure that is a part of parenthood. I saw that I was going to keep doing things wrong, making mistakes, but I would still be a mother, the only kind of mother I knew how to be. And somehow through these efforts I would be a good mother.

I faced a few more facts. I would never be the "room mom" type at

school, the stalwart volunteer, one of the committed women who orga-
nize special fund-raising activities and school fairs, who sit on commit-
tees and bake brownies and make macadamia-nut brittle and three-level
chip dip and chili for bake sales, and address envelopes and light up the
phone tree and hang Christmas and prom decorations. Over the years
I've done a modicum of volunteering (as well as teaching informal creative writing sessions to kids), but I stopped feeling guilty about not
being a familiar face in Annie's classroom (even when confronted with
the occasional overly zealous Room Mom hinting to me that I'm not at
school enough). I've talked to Annie about this parenting "lapse," and she
says she doesn't mind. She goes to school, she says, to learn things, to be
with teachers and classmates. I am with her at home.

And I *am* with her at home. I made the decision early on. Because her
father is absent a good deal, I am the mainstay. There are things I miss because of this decision, events I can't make, but I don't mind.

Now that my daughter has just turned fifteen, I reapproach this
question of "looking away." Why did (does) that image seem so implic-
itly wrong, such an indictment? I realize now that almost every aspect
of motherhood in our culture is symbolic—from the image of the
madonna to the mindless commercials selling squeaky-clean airbrushed
moms.

We see mothers a certain way. And what we see is that they are
seeing us. The constant gaze of the mother on us is imperative. That is
why if she is caught looking away, she is betraying us, betraying childhood, betraying the whole social "moral" structure that reinforces limits
on her behavior. If she is looking away, it means that she has a self—and
traditionally, motherhood and self-hood do not go together.

Am I still guilty? Of course. That mother bird (or her descendant) still builds her nest outside my bedroom window in the cypress tree; but these days Annie is usually in her own room and doesn't hear Ms. Swallow or her peepers. But sometimes my daughter comes into my bedroom and says nothing. She comes in just to sit next to me and read. We sit quietly, the two of us, "turned away" from each other, flipping pages, engrossed, but right next to each other, close. The sky outside the windows turns violet, darkens. The moon rises. We smile at our separate stories. The mother bird and her babies chirp. We read on.

Choice

ANNALIESE HOOD

Wind tongues the small panes of glass beside the bed. I sit on the edge of the mattress, my daughter's body a lump quivering under the worn quilt, her face in the pillow. The sleet continues to click at the silence.

"Mom," she says.

"I'm here," I answer.

"Sometimes I see her."

"Did you see her tonight?" I know exactly where she has been in her head. It started when she was six. When we argue, she sometimes imagines white picket fences and matching plates and a well-coiffed birth mother.

"She wore a mint green apron, like a bib with ruffles over her shoulders. Under it was a green dress. Velvet, I think. With gold buttons. I could see them at the bottom of her dress."

Tamara pokes her head out from under the pile of covers.

"I couldn't see her face," she adds.

She never can.

"I bet it was gorgeous," I say.

I look down at my jeans and an old woolen sweater, a light dusting of flour on the left sleeve. I am not the perfect mother my daughter envisions. The mother she is reconstructing is someone with whom she never lived, someone she saw only twice in the foster home she lived in for two years before she came north in a borrowed black Ford.

I am the mother who brushes damp maple branches from the path, balancing a kerosene lamp on the way to the outhouse. I am the mother who hauls the wood, buckets the water, and measures flour for tofu pie or invented cookie recipes. I am the mother who tips over chairs and drapes sheets to create caverns for play. I am the mother who boogies shoeless to Joan Armatrading and Arnett Cobb and Smokey Robinson, twirling a child wildly. I am the mother who cries over Madame Butterfly.

The fact that my daughter has another mother somewhere seems quite normal and quite strange, but the truth is it affects our lives not at all. The bigger truth is I couldn't have birthed a more appropriate daughter: I am her mother, just as she is my child.

Becca, a neighbor down the road, ruffles Tamara's hair, gives her a hug, sends her off to play with her Nicky. She turns to me and says in her soft voice, "Oh, she is so sweet."

"I love her so much," I say. I know if I were to step outside my body, I would see a beaming me, the proverbial red heart pulsing through my pilly sweater.

Becca smiles. "I know, but she's not your real child. You can't love her as much as your own."

Real versus what? Imaginary? Dammit, she is my own, I want to say. My gut wrenches at comments like this, but I hold back. I know Becca means no harm, and my relationship with my child has nothing to do with anyone else's perception of it.

She is my daughter. Of course, I love her as much. Sometimes, I have feared, even more.

I smile and explain calmly, "Honest to God, Bec, it's the same." I know she doesn't believe me. But until someone reminds me, I never think of my child as having come from a different world, a different place, a different womb with unknown sperm and unknown egg. My child is very real and very much mine, no matter that she came from a different body in a different state with different genes.

Just as many people assume—although most would never acknowledge it—that children who join a family through adoption occupy a position of lesser value or identity or status in that family, they also often assume that people adopt because they can't give birth themselves. Adoption actually was a first choice for us. Pregnancy just made it happen second. With over a quarter of a million children living in foster care in the United States, we knew that children already had been born who needed us.

The first time I saw Tamara she was a two-year-old child with chocolate-colored ringlets. Wearing a red jacket exposing her delicate wrists, she stood beside a two-foot-by-one-foot box of all her belongings and offered me a face so sadly sweet I was afraid to kiss her. My daughter is the town's first black resident and my second child.

The first is seven months younger than she. Tanek was seized from a neat, seemingly too small incision just above my pubic bone in an April when the snows had eaten gravel from the culvert and substituted a raw wound of frigid water for a dirt road bed. A child with apple-red cheeks suitable for polishing, sand-colored hair that brushes the small of his back, and an insistence on telling the truth, he began life small and meconium-covered. When he first met his sister, he threw his pudgy arms around her, and they have done an arhythmic dance of holding and hugging and pushing away ever since.

Do they fight? Sure. Are these fights colored by more than those in other families? No. Do they love each other, hate each other, help each other, thwart each other's plans, and soothe each other's fears and apprehensions? All of the above. That's what family is.

I am the mother who is all things to Tanek, with no shadow thoughts in the background, no escape plans for a better life. This mother is the only mother. He wishes sometimes he could invent a father other than the one he has. This father stuck around for years, but he has never been much of a parent. Always too busy, always somewhere else, always consumed with what he wants to do. He promises swing sets. He promises time. He promises he will not yell anymore. They are only promises.

I used to believe that if you choose to adopt a child, no matter what it takes, you must fulfill all promises. But as with other things, the child seized from my womb and the child who slid into daylight through another's birth canal get the same deal. Some promises we can fulfill. Some we choose not to. And others are just unfillable. And so I become mother and father to everyone.

Home is Mt. Chase, Maine, population 164. It is a snowsled-riding, hunter-logger community. Maine is the second-whitest white-bread state in the country, but this town never blinked at me and mine. They smiled at a child who insisted on wearing his underpants on the outside when he was three. And often I swear these small-town folk saw no color when it came to one of theirs, and that's what the Hood kids were. They were theirs, just like the McCarthys and the Craigs and the Carvers.

No, *nigger* was not an unheard word, but it was a word quickly squelched.

"Chuckie called you a name on the bus, Tamara?" asks the principal.

"Yes," the make-no-waves second-grade daughter says quietly.

"Do you want to tell me what it was?"

"No," she says.

"Was it 'nigger'?"

"Yes," the small voice answers.

"I'm sorry. It won't happen again."

And I'll be damned, it didn't.

To me this family is like any other with joy and pain and wounds raw enough to bleed if rubbed too hard. To me this family is not about adoption but about the extraordinary people that make it weather and survive and thrive.

Honestly, a black child was not the strangest thing about us. It is far stranger to our neighbors that we are vegetarians than that our family includes an adopted child. In the second grade Mrs. Carroll tells Tanek he will die if he continues to be a vegetarian. He tells her George Bernard Shaw did quite well. She sends him to the principal's office. It is far stranger to be a third-grade atheist—black or white—in a town with a rabid, foot-stomping Pentecostal church; a Methodist church; one Catholic, a Jehovah's Witness, a small Seventh-Day Adventist congregation, the Baptists a few miles down the road; and a Cub Scout troop that Tanek would not lie for. It is far stranger that we have no television than that we have an adopted child and that she happens to be black. Our children just make us more visible in a town where we have always been more visible.

We live in a quirky, jerry-built home that sports early American insulation, a welded barrel stove pumping out heat in winter and holding vases of daisies and delphiniums in summer, stapled cloth on Sheetrocked walls, a hand pump in the kitchen, and barn boards torn from the leavings of other people's lives. A tree trunk supports the kitchen counter. An eighty-year-old neighbor says elephants could mate and the floors would hold.

Tamara wants things in order. Tanek doesn't care. He saves pinecones and pebbles. She tucks the play pans under the counter, wipes the tables, and tells her brother, "No, don't touch," in a very touchable home. Some might suggest that she is like this because her foster parents kept her confined to a small room with a television and a couch; the rest of the house was off limits. Some might surmise her behavior is genetic. The why doesn't matter to me. She is my daughter. And my daughter likes order. For whatever reason.

Tamara's adoption paves the way for her brother Arrick, the town's second black resident—the child with the strong face, spindly legs, and piano fingers, who bruises my shins under a restaurant table in Columbus, Ohio, while he daintily blots his two-year-old lips with a napkin as I sign the placement papers his social worker slides across the Formica tabletop. Two plane rides and a two-hour drive later, he greets his five-year-old brother and his six-year-old sister by smacking them in the face with a Matchbox Rolls-Royce.

The weather is good for his arrival: a mild fall, sweet apple-scented wind, no turmoil. The life, however, is stormy.

He is my macaroni-and-cheese-out-of-the-box boy. The one that brings me to highs and lows I never imagined possible—including when he steals a gun and tells his third-grade classmates he will need it in New York City to hunt for food when he leaves us.

Arrick can step over a bleeding person and merely look inquisitively at the scenario—the placement of a curled finger, the lay of the palm, the lips, a detached observer at two or five or nine. He arrives with no observable thread of empathy and continues to walk a line that teeters on the edge of immorality. I labor over empathy, sympathy, even plain old caring. The boundaries between right and wrong blur; he often sticks in the gray area no matter what I do.

When he is three, I realize how seriously he pushes touch away, uncomfortable being its focus, and so I decide to respect his space. I am a space respecter by nature. I cannot easily hug him or kiss him. Sometimes I am lucky: He forgets and puts his arm around me softly, almost gently, his voice climbing and shooting and winging itself in conversation.

This works until he is seven. I am angry and so is he. I cannot recall what has happened.

"You don't love me as much as you love Tanek and Tamara," he gulps.

I am shocked.

"Why would you say that, Arrick?" I ask.

"Because you don't hug and kiss me as much as you do them."

And so I begin again to maul and slobber and touch. And he continues to push and scowl and rebuff. I am thick-skinned.

I am the mother who has marked every time he said "I love you" in a notebook. There are five entries. He is the child who never thinks about mothers—present or past, birth or adopted, real or imagined. Some might speculate that this son of mine is emotionally distant because he spent the first two years of his life alone in a crib, barely touched, playing with the wrinkles in the sheet or the folds in his diaper. Some might believe that he has inherited this distance thing, but I think he could just as easily have stolen the gun if I had watched him slip out from between my own thighs. Who knows? Who cares? I only care that he opens a little, softens his hard exterior to let the light kiss of those who dearly love him penetrate the surface of his dark skin. He is mine, and I want him to know that I love him for all that he is.

People ask, "Why black children?" The answer is, "Not black children. Children. And they are black." These were our criteria: any sex, any race, any religion, no serious mental or physical problems, and under the age of five.

Shani was to have been child number three, just before Arrick. In a playground in Mattapoisett, Massachusetts, this two-year-old son of a Nigerian prince stares through my solid body as if it were thin glass. His eyes are hollow. His broad unsmiling lips are set. I am so uncertain, fearful actually. I push down the lump in my throat.

I juggle fear and love with the arrival of each child, adopted or birthed. Even those who know me best don't know this about me. The fear has been so sharp and deep sometimes that I cannot keep a journal because I only trust myself to put down inanities, simplistic reactions.

I know that something is very wrong, but I take this new son the four hundred miles home to meet his brother and sister. Shani sleeps in the Chinese-red crib that had been Tanek's. All night I hear him bang his head against the headboard. That explains the bald patch he came with. They said he liked to play with pan covers. They did not say he spins them top-like for hours and hours on end. I drive forty-five minutes to the library and take out books. I read in all those hours I cannot sleep until I find the description that matches his behaviors and no longer think I am crazy. I wrestle with my badness, my inability to handle all of this that is Shani.

Choice

How do I give back a child? How do I give back my children's brother? How do I say that an adopted child is no different to me than a birthed one, and yet also say autism is too much?

In the end all I can say is that I understand how parents disembowel themselves for their children, and sometimes that disembowelment means giving them up, back, away. All I can say is that my children now understand that sometimes when a parent does what's best for a child and for a family, it's unfathomable to the rest of the world. It is beyond the words I know. No health insurance, a rocky car. The closest facility for Shani was two hundred miles away. We make painful choices in a life. Some we regret. All we must live with.

I will always remember lifting my hollow-eyed son into the arms of his caseworker in the backseat of a taxi in Boston.

Ten months later Arrick arrives. He slips into the rhythm of family routines, including the drawing of straws for after-dinner jobs: a washer, a dryer, a putter-awayer, and, most important now, a storyteller. I pour steaming water into dishpans. We begin.

The stories are a necessity, transporting us to parallel worlds. Tanek describes a boy driving an imaginary tofu truck, rattling down a starless, frost-heaved dirt road, his new brother laughing at his side; Tamara tells about the matching pink china plates a little girl would have had if she had stayed with her first mother; Arrick explains how a small boy hides from the wolf spiders on a misty evening, their webs like white hammocks full of wings. Their third-person stories are always about them.

I don't know how all our stories will turn out: which word makes the most significant impact, which harshness damages, which one strengthens, which chrysalis signifies a turning point. I do know that I will continue to listen to the stories, forgive the unforgivable, sing off-key silly under the northern lights, and love these children, the one born of my body and the three not, as fiercely mine as the one who chewed on my nipple, even Shani who went away.

Driving

JON KATZ

The Prince of Rides rode forth for the final time on a warm spring day, the last of the school year. He was approaching, by his reckoning, roughly the one hundred thousandth mile of ferrying his daughter and her friends and classmates around town, around northern New Jersey, around a not-insignificant chunk of the northeastern United States.

His daughter and the other kids had never given much thought to the way they were transported from here to there. Somebody else made the arrangements, and cars equipped with cheerful drivers magically appeared when required. All that the young passengers had to do was climb inside and buckle up; there was no reason for them to understand the pressures, responsibilities, complexities, or technical details.

But the Prince, nostalgically recalling the ten years since he had left corporate life and begun spending a major chunk of each week as an unpaid chauffeur, understood very well. In his long reign, driving his child and others, singly and in batches, he had never forgotten a kid, never left one behind, never even kept one waiting for more than a minute or two.

At first in an aging sedan, then in a proud Volvo station wagon, and now in this minivan—the school carpool was growing, and so were the kids it carried and the size of their backpacks—he had made it through on time in swirling blizzards and deafening thunderstorms and freezing rain.

Though there had been some near-misses, the Prince was usually the only one who noticed. His daughter and her fellow passengers simply yakked on about Cabbage Patch dolls and birthday parties and the inexplicable behavior of boys.

He knew that soon his daughter would be able to drive herself, and then she and her friends would be free of him and his van for good. Probably, after a year or two, they'd forget completely about the Prince and his rides. It wasn't the sort of contribution history noted.

* * *

People roll their eyes when they talk about the ceaseless driving required of parents, in much the way they grump about lousy weather. I see it differently. Driving was always an opportunity for me, a dad who wanted to be closer to his child than the dads he saw growing up got to be to theirs.

Perhaps because I live in New Jersey, whose state symbol ought to be the steel-belted radial, I've come to see driving as serious stuff, with important traditions, challenges, and rules. I took it seriously and did it well. I glowed the time a Soccer Mom, formidable in her towering sports utility vehicle, praised my punctuality, my contented passengers, my safety record. "You're the Prince of Rides," she anointed me.

It wasn't unheard of for a man to be doing so much driving, but it was rare. "Doesn't your daddy work?" one of my daughter's friends whispered to her in the back of the van one day.

"No," she whispered back. "He's a writer." Real work was something people dressed up and left home to do; sitting in a basement office clacking away at a keyboard all day didn't qualify.

$\mathcal{D}$riving

Since my wife rarely drove the carpool and disliked driving in general, many of my daughter's friends probably assumed that her father was not only unemployed but divorced.

But I considered myself deeply fortunate. Part of what had propelled me out of an intensely pressured media job was the chance to do exactly this: the everyday scut work, the chores, the ceaseless drop off and pick up.

My own parents weren't around much when I was a kid. It's astonishing how little they knew about my life. My father, in particular, seemed to spend much of his later years in a vain effort to try to catch up.

Who were your friends? he asked when I was thirty, thirty-five, forty. Were you happy in school? Did you like sports? When did you become a reader? My adulthood was a complex code he was never able to crack. Somehow it was too late; there was too much lost ground to cover.

That was not going to be my fate, I had sworn early. I was going to write a different history. My daughter wouldn't be a stranger to me. I would know who her friends were, whether she was happy in school or liked sports; I'd know the moment she became a reader. I never wanted to find myself trying to figure out who she was decades down the road. I would spare her and me the cruel fate of men who are often perpetual strangers to their families.

Driving helped.

The debris that accumulated in the van bore testament to my years on the road with my kid. The gum and candy wrappers, toll receipts, tufts of dog hair, long-lost school papers and misplaced toys were maps and memories, clues to part of my child's life and of my life with her.

If I could, I'd have driven the van into the basement and left it there for twenty years or so so that I could return from time to time, slide open the doors, and bring her childhood back to life. Here is where she tearfully consoled herself with a Fudgsicle after losing a friend; here in the back is where we stuffed the new two-wheeler after her first bike ride. That's where a flying rock dinged the fender on that long, rutted dirt road up to camp.

We drove to art classes and singing lessons. To the library for homework projects, to the drugstore chain for school supplies. To toy stores and video arcades and beaches. To pediatricians' offices and the emergency room.

We drove deep into New Jersey to stables, into Manhattan for plays and museum visits, to Cape Cod for family vacations, to the shore for romps on the boardwalk and carnival rides. We drove to play dates at the homes of friends who invariably lived fifteen miles away.

En route, we concocted innumerable games and rituals to spice up our drives; once invented, they lived for years. We looked for Rock People lurking by the roadside, Tree Monsters that might pounce on the car. Ordinary suburban landmarks became dramatic: the way home from the mall led over three hills: Werewolf's, Witches', and Dracula's.

There was something moving and connecting about all the time we spent in cars, gliding gently from one lane to the next, tires hissing along rainsoaked highways, me preoccupied with traffic and weather, she in her own universe, safe and oblivious as kids are in cars. Having no real idea of what could happen, they put themselves completely in the driver's hands. They relax.

And sometimes they even talk.

$\mathcal{D}$riving

*   *   *

Communication, I've learned, is actually nurtured while driving kids around. Somehow the driver becomes invisible while conversation rages all around him. The same girls who will respond monosyllabically to any question you dare to raise talk with rare abandon in the backseat. The ethical response, I initially decided, was to put on a CD and try not to listen. But the chatter, the choruses of glee and heartache, the observations were sometimes far too compelling.

"I'm so sad," M announced one afternoon. "My hamster killed herself last night. She threw herself right off the dresser and onto the floor in front of my cat." J recounted in amazing, graphic detail how she'd thrown up in class.

From behind the wheel I always knew which toy was going to take off at Christmas, which cartoon was rising and which getting stale, what new fashion or food craze was sweeping the youth market. I learned which teachers were loving and understanding, which harsh and forbidding. Which kids were popular, which were goats.

Now and then a kid would stagger into the car after school looking so forlorn and discouraged, I wondered what could possibly have happened. Sometimes someone would volunteer: Somebody made fun of her pigtails. A teacher was thoughtlessly cruel or critical. She didn't get a part in the play. Her best friend was suddenly sitting at another table in the cafeteria.

I heard lurid and shocking things. C peed in her pants during recess. G talked nasty and was teaching the entire second grade the f-word. N cheated during Capture the Flag.

By and large I treated such anecdotes as top secret. If kids started getting grilled by their parents about their carpool chatter, conversation would dry up. Only once did I violate privilege—when one of my young passengers cried so painfully and for so long on the way home that it alarmed me. Her parents, it turned out, were getting divorced.

If we rarely divulged specific conversations, the carpool parents sometimes traded important information—who might be feeling lonely or defeated by multiplication or terrified of soccer practice. If we all understood that the kids were entitled to privacy, we also extended the occasional heads-up—a sort of professional courtesy—when we saw things that other parents needed to know.

The other kind of communication flourishes on wheels, too, for some reason—the one-on-one variety. If you shut up and listen, your kid talks to you. If you stop asking stupid questions, she'll volunteer what you want to know. Even in silence there is powerful connection.

One evening, driving home from an overnight at a faraway friend's house, we ran into a snow squall that swiftly covered the road and began to send drifts blowing across the landscape. I considered pulling over, but it was already late, and visibility was so poor that somebody might well plow into us.

So I drove cautiously on, even though I sometimes had to lean out the window to follow the white lines along the highway.

I glanced over at my daughter. She seemed more fascinated than anxious, sitting silently as I crawled along and prayed that I wouldn't veer off the road. The drive took more than an hour, and we never spoke during that time, yet we had rarely felt closer. I loved the absolute trust she afforded me—it didn't seem to occur to her that I couldn't navigate the storm and bring her safely home—and I was determined not to betray it.

$\mathcal{D}riving$

"This is so neat," she said quietly as our suburban dogsled, enveloped by snow and ice, crept slowly through the keening winds. So it was.

On these countless trips we grew closer, mile by mile, toll booth by toll booth. We talked about my childhood basset hound and how he would push me out of bed in the middle of the night to make more room for himself. She confided stories about the social cruelty of children, dramas I rarely heard otherwise. We rehearsed roles in school plays, prepped for tests. Over candy bars, sodas, and gummy chew things, I discussed the projects I was working on, and once in a while she was even interested. Side by side, relieved of the burden of eye contact, often shrouded in darkness, we got into the habit of making conversation, money in the bank for any father and child.

Women often take such closeness with their children for granted; men know better. Kids instinctively gravitate to mothers, their anchors, their pole stars. Mothers connote safety, stability, comfort; Dads often have to work at it.

Driving gave me a way to cross into that other sphere, a connection that developed on the road and then transcended it and became woven into our relationship for good.

"Dad, are you always happy? Do you ever get scared?" my daughter musingly asked one night as we were driving home from some school event. I was keeping a wary eye on the giant tractor trailers cruising in front of and behind me.

It was not a casual question and not the kind that parents often discuss with elementary schoolers. I had no idea where it came from, but for just a bit she and I pondered contentment and anxiety, the pull between what you yearned to do and what you needed to do. After she had listened closely for three minutes or so, I could see her attention wander.

The conversation was drifting, as it so often does with parents, into a speech. So I stopped talking, wondering at the question and the talk that would probably never have arisen at the dinner table.

* * *

"Aren't you looking forward to the day when she can drive herself?" a neighbor asked, standing nearby as the van backed out of its garage berth for the zillionth time and prepared to ascend still another highway.

"You bet," the Prince said, chuckling back.

And it was almost true. The good parent works to make him- or herself obsolete. Wasn't the point of the exercise to help her drive happily away one day, under her own steam, toward her own life?

But the Prince would miss his time behind the wheel. He was never more elemental and important. He would always remember the pigtailed little kid in the seat beside him, slurping her magenta Slush Puppy.

His daughter remembered, too, he was surprised to learn. The other evening, as the Prince brought her home from a sweaty workout at the gym—she was on a mission to get fit for a summer trip to Europe—she suddenly emerged from a reverie and noticed where they were. "Hey," she announced. "This is Witches' Hill! And there," she added, pointing to an ordinary local church, "there's Dracula's Castle. The lights are on. He's awake!"

Five Snapshots from the Year Jake Turned Ten

ROBERTA ISRAELOFF

After an interminable Little League game on a chilly May evening, Jake, my ten-year-old son, wants to get ice cream. We tell him that it's late and we have to go home so he can do his homework, take a shower, and get into bed. He throws himself into the backseat of the car, refuses to say a word when we try to congratulate him on his game—as a first-time pitcher, he gave up a scant two runs—stalks into the house, chucks his mud-clogged sneakers down the stairs, bangs the broom and dust pan when I make him sweep up the mess, storms into his room, and slams the door.

Fifteen minutes later I go in to say good night, and he asks me to leave. "Dad and I have a rule," I tell him. "We don't go to bed angry." I bend down to peck him on his cheek.

Instantly one hand flies to his face; he spits in it and begins furiously wiping the point of our contact as if he had been stung by a wasp, eradicating not only any residue of my kiss but its very existence.

Gasping, face flushed, I walk into the bathroom and close the door. You ungrateful little shit, I think to myself, my eyes brimming with tears.

185

What happened to my sweet boy who loves nothing more than to have me sit by his side while he strokes my cheek? It's as if he's turning into a teenager. And then it strikes me: He is.

Of course. Now it all makes sense: his moodiness, his snotty back talk; the way he wastes time in the bathroom combing and recombing his hair, scrutinizes his clothes, talks about girls late into the night when he has sleepovers. He's on the cusp of being a preteen. When my older son, now sixteen, went through these changes, I had been mystified and anxious but also relieved. Each threshold he crossed left me weak with relief that the process wasn't stalled, that he was moving forward, illuminating the way, as pioneers do, on a journey tinged with the vivifying thrill of the unexplored. Now I know what's ahead. And I know this is the last time I'll be passing through. Jake is giving me a preview of the rest of my life when I will be bereft not only of him, my youngest child, but of children.

*　*　*

"Next September when you're in sixth grade, you'll have your own key to the house," I told Jake. It had been a balmy April evening, and we were sitting in the car outside the middle school he would be attending in a few months. From the gym came sounds of music—this was the first mixer to which the fifth graders were invited—but Jake showed no signs of being ready to mix. Slightly slumped in his seat but very composed, he looked out the window, studying the kids milling outside the building and the building itself, so much bigger than his womblike elementary school. I imagined that he was trying to picture how he would insert himself into the ongoing scenario. He was surveying his prospects, calculating when to make his move.

"That way," I continued, "when you get home from school, you can just let yourself in even if I'm not there yet." I was already planning to spend more time in the city without worrying about having to meet Jake's bus. He had been looking forward to this privilege for years.

And so was I. In fact, sometimes I thought the end of his childhood hadn't come a moment too soon. I was tired of sitting through class plays. I no longer had the attention span to build Legos rocket ships with him. I wanted more time for myself, for my marriage, for my work. Some of my friends, confronting this transition, ran out to buy kittens or puppies, or took jobs in nursery schools. For me, nothing was less appealing. Jake was on the move, and I was too—not backward into another nursery but ahead to discover how to be the mother of a preteen, a teenager, a young adult.

I looked at Jake's hands, folded on his lap. When he was a toddler, he used to play elaborate games with his fingers, interlocking and releasing them in various patterns. He also had a small bald spot that the doctor thought might have been caused by stress. Jake looked anything but stressed now. This big, raucous school riveted his considerable attention but didn't faze him. He had friends; he trusted he would do well in class; he was eager to try out for band and for the basketball team. In his profile I saw the face of the mature man he was on his way to becoming.

When he saw one of his friends walking down the block, Jake calmly opened the car door and left without saying good-bye, without so much as a look in my direction. Both boys were tall and shaped like bean poles—they hadn't yet begun to acquire volume and heft—but they gamely put their hands in their pants pockets the way their older brothers did, and together they walked toward the gym where the girls were.

*   *   *

Four-thirty in the afternoon I was in my study, trying to make an impossible deadline. Jake knocked on the door and came inside. "Can I practice pitching with you?"

I tried to glance at the clock so he wouldn't notice, but knew that he did. I had hoped to have this assignment finished by dinner time. "Okay," I told him. I would have to work until bed if I stopped now and I would probably pass a sleepless night from the accumulating anxiety, but if I had learned anything in the past ten years, it was that I would rather suffer the momentary pang of undone work than the heartsickness I always felt after declining an invitation to play. All too soon the invitations would cease. And I was sure I'd miss them.

We threw the ball around for about fifteen minutes, and then Jake said he had enough. But I hadn't. It was a beautiful March afternoon, and I felt elated to be outside with my son.

"You know," I told Jake as we sat together on the porch, "when you were a baby, we spent nearly every moment together."

"No, we didn't," he said. I was so taken aback that I didn't speak for several seconds.

"Of course we did," I answered him.

"No," he insisted. "I went to day care and nursery school."

"You were in day care for a total of six hours a week," I told him. How many times had I calculated those hours, trying to assuage my conscience that I wasn't away too much? "And at nursery school two half-days until you were three, and then three half-days."

"And I had a baby-sitter," he said stubbornly.

"Four hours a week," I said, remembering how I would retreat into my study when she came, desperately trying to stay awake long enough to finish an assignment, grade some papers, return some phone calls, balance a checkbook. And suddenly the weight of all the books I didn't read or write, the letters I failed to answer, the job prospects I passed up, the movies and concerts I didn't go to, the nights and mornings my husband and I didn't make love, the summers we didn't fly to Paris, the Everest of everything I didn't do so I could be the kind of mother I wanted to be appeared in front of me, crushing me with its sheer mass.

And for what? Evidently the hours I had spent anguishing about my time away from Jake were wasted hours. According to the myth Jake had composed, and which he'd recite for himself, his girlfriends, and his children, I had left him to go to work. I might as well have. Maybe I should have. Nothing was clear except the startling fact that I no longer owned the script to my son's childhood.

*   *   *

Finding myself with an unexpected half-hour on a February afternoon between one meeting and the next, more than enough time to buy a gift for my cousin's first child, I headed over to Macy's in Herald Square. Sixteen years ago, just before my oldest son was born, I had come here with my mother to buy a layette. Now I took the escalator to the sixth floor and began the long walk toward the back of the store: through the teenage department; then sizes 8 to 20, where Jake now shopped; through 6 and 6X, that odd size, the first size I remember applying to me as a girl; then through toddlers—this was turning into an archaeological expedition, a walk into the deep recesses of time past— until finally, nestled into the far corner, I entered the section for infants.

Briskly, for I was in a rush, I surveyed the tables and racks of mer-
chandise, noting the new baby paraphernalia on the market—variously
colored carriers and car seats with snappy zippers and Velcro. But I was
drawn to a wall display of dressing gowns, the kind with drawstrings that
you use for two or three weeks and never again. I had saved one that both
sons had used, a sturdy flannel hand-me-down from a neighbor, yellow
with a floral pattern. The one on the rack was gossamer white. I fingered
it. So soft. So impossibly tiny. Not at all practical as a gift.

And the next thing I knew I was ambushed by tears. Within moments
I was sobbing. The floor was nearly deserted, thank God, and the few
saleswomen knew enough to scurry away. Maybe they were used to the
sight of middle-aged women breaking down while contemplating baby
gowns, but my reaction stunned me beyond words. Worst of all, the tears
wouldn't stop. Even as I roused myself to move and made my way
through the department like a blind person, fingering everything—
gowns, stuffed pandas, blankets, snowsuits—I felt entirely lost, clutching
at remnants of a lost world, which indeed they were.

How warm was Jake's head when I cradled it in my palm? How
much heft did his body have? How exactly did he grunt as he settled
down to nurse? The answers were gone, vanished. I could summon pictures and words but couldn't retrieve the tactile treasure of him. My
memories were devoid of sensual content. I couldn't smell or taste or
hear them. They existed in one flat dimension—the past.

As I collected myself enough to buy a stuffed animal, I found myself
wondering if we ever get over the fact that our children grow old, clam
up, go off on their own, need us less and less. I felt as if I were gestating in
reverse—shrinking, pulling back—so that Jake could move on, so that

we could navigate our next joint passage: his to teenagerhood, mine to middle and then old age.

*   *   *

"Mom," Jake calls. About fifteen minutes have elapsed since he scrubbed my kiss from his face. "Can you come here?"

I put aside my crossword puzzle, walk into his room, and sit down on his bed. "I can't stay angry at you," he says, his arms encircling my neck, drawing me down to his impossibly downy cheek, toasty from bed.

We snuggle, and I don't want to let him go. I know the frequency of these snuggle sessions will diminish. Soon he'll barely be in the mood to say good night to me. These sensations—of his skin, his hair, the sound of his breathing—will vanish, just as his baby sensations have. One day soon, I know from experience, he will be able to stay angry at me. He will be able to work up a fury and sustain it for days, even weeks, at a low boil.

But he is not there yet. He is practicing. Though silver threads still yoke our nervous systems, and always will, they'll soon be stretched to the breaking point. What Jake and I are beginning, I realize, are our negotiations. Our common border is in question; there will be skirmishes. We have to figure out how much to give away, how much to keep. Love isn't always enough, and it is never simple. Biological, primal, yes, but never uncomplicated, not from the first breath.

I give him a kiss and start to get up. He tugs at my hand. "I want my baba," he says. He means his milk bottle. We've had this conversation before. He's perfectly serious.

"Bottles are for babies," I tell him.

191

"I want to be a baby again," he says. "I want to get into bed between you and Daddy, right in the middle, and suck my milk. Warm milk. You used to warm it for me, remember?"

I remember. Oh, God, I remember the sweet-smelling yeasty loaf of him snuggling next to us, contentedly slurping, lost in his own reverie.

"I felt so secure then," he says with a sighs and with more wistfulness than a ten-year-old should possess.

"Well, I'm not going to buy you a bottle," I say. I don't tell him that I have one stashed away in the back of the kitchen cupboard that I couldn't bear to discard.

"Why not?" he asks, his eyes wide and innocent.

Every answer I can think of is ludicrous. Because you're too old. Because you won't like it. Why don't I just go to the store and buy him a bottle, fill it with milk, and let him discover how attenuated the flow is and how unsatisfactory? Don't I want him to be disillusioned, to find out that it isn't really what he wants? Or am I afraid that he'll love it, that he'll never grow up as he must, as I want him to, as I want him not to. Of what am I most afraid? There is no logical answer.

"I want my baba," he says again. In his face I see the man he'll become and the baby he was. I see myself as a baby and as the old woman I am on my way to becoming. Babies transform time. Children, if you listen to them closely, give you a window on your own soul, your own deepest chaotic illogical desires—to be a grown-up and a baby, to be in charge and be submissive, to want everything at once and nothing more than a bottle of warm milk. Having children is the most illuminating and subversive act I have ever perpetrated.

Jake sighs. He pulls the covers up to his neck and turns to the wall. This is how he prepares for sleep, by pulling away from me, into himself.

"Well, I still want it," he says. Though the urgency is gone, though he knows he won't have his bottle, he is not quite ready to stop asking for it. We'll find a way out of this conversation one of these days. I'm in no hurry.

Taking Wing

LARRY BROWN

number of things run through your mind when your children graduate from school. We were here four years ago with Billy Ray, and we were excited, happy, proud, and sad. Today we're doing the same thing with Shane, knowing that in two more months he'll be leaving home to go to college. As I sit here thinking about how things have changed, I notice that everything in the coliseum has stayed the same: the Southeastern Conference flags hanging from the high ceiling, the blue and red seats, the smell of fresh popcorn. Probably the only thing that has changed is that there are several more coats of wax on the hardwood floor.

The time goes by so fast when they're little, and you don't notice how fast the days are seeping away. Maybe you're so busy with living and what you're doing that you don't have time to notice. But one day you see that they're spreading their wings like the fledgling bluebirds that nest in boxes in the backyard. When it comes, you don't want it. When they were little, you kept thinking, One of these days I'll have time for the things I want to do, need to do. Selfishness, I guess. From the moment they come home from the hospital, you get busy and you stay busy. Diapers to change, bottles to make, the hours walking with them over your shoulder, the way their hair smells—and all your time is given to this helpless child that you brought into the world.

Billy Ray went away to college, and it was only forty miles from home. I hated to see him leave. But maybe when you have three, it's easier to let go of the first one, knowing that two more are still at home. Plenty more time until they're gone. Wrong.

It gradually creeps up again, the little signs that it's going to take place again: class rings, the prom, ordering senior pictures and graduation invitations, another one measured for cap and gown. You knew it was coming, but why doesn't it just slow down?

That day is here again. All those little boys and girls that have been a part of your life are now dressed in red gowns with white collars, the caps with their gold tassels swinging. The music starts for their final march to what they *know* is the beginning of their freedom. They feel grown, and rightly so. They come out one at a time to find the last seat they will sit in as a high school student—all the boys with smiles on their faces, and some of the girls with tears in their eyes. You watch for a sign that he sees the two of you, a little wave that says, Hey, Mama. Hey, Daddy. I made it. It's the same little wave he gave as he climbed on the school bus on the first day of school, except this time the hand is that of a man. Almost.

Billy Ray was a different child from Shane. Billy Ray never gave us any problems in school. He was always willing to do right. He had lots of friends and stayed busy doing boy things. Shane had lots of friends, too, but they took their fun a little more seriously. We got called to the school for a teacher-parent meeting quite often. There was a group of them that stuck together all the time. If one was in trouble, they were all in trouble.

We should have known that Shane was going to be harder to raise than Billy Ray. The first sign should have been when it was suggested that he not come back to the school after his first semester in kindergarten. We had dropped Shane off at the place, and he didn't want to stay. We went through this every morning, but this day was a little different. As I was leaving, I heard him running toward me. I just kept walking, a hard thing to do. I figured the teacher would get to him, and they would begin some activity to get his mind off wanting to leave with us. The next sound was this loud thump. I turned around, and there lay his teacher on the floor. He had somehow flipped her over his shoulder. School just wasn't his favorite place to be. He liked his teachers, but he didn't want to be told or asked to do anything—by anybody.

The day we've been dreading comes too quickly. The sun is shining brightly when we get up. Boxes are everywhere in the living room, packed with all the things he'll need or thinks he'll need to start life as a college freshman. Everybody is here. Girlfriends, too. Mary Annie and I just look around, moving slowly, not wanting to hurry, not wanting to start this day, knowing that when we come back tonight, it will not be the same, that part of the nest will be missing and broken, another new adjustment to make.

We pull out of the driveway with Shane and Kim leading the way. They are not going to like being separated after all this time together— two years now. Mary Annie and I follow with our daughter, LeAnne, in the car with us, Billy Ray and his girlfriend, Paula, following us for the two-hour drive down to Starkville, Mississippi. It's going to take all of us to get Shane into his room. Mary Annie drives while I read. LeAnne sits quietly in the backseat, only leaning up once in a while to change the station on the radio. LeAnne and Shane have always been close. He was the one who played with her when she was little. His was the shoulder she cried on instead of mine. This is going to be hard on her.

When we finally get there, Shane goes to check in, and we start unpacking. Billy Ray and I groan when we find out the couch will have to be carried up to the fourth floor. But after a couple of hours, everything is in the room. It just needs to be organized. I sit down on the couch for a breather. The halls are full of students and parents looking just as bewildered as all of us. This is his home now. I have to get used to that fact. But I feel like crying.

It's time to leave. The good-byes are said and the hugs are given. Mary Annie doesn't start crying until she's halfway across the parking lot, almost to the car. It's hard to leave him down here all by himself, but we've known it was coming for quite a while.

When we get home, everything is quiet. LeAnne goes to her room and gets on the telephone, as usual. Billy Ray goes to Paula's. I go to my office, and Mary Annie sits in the living room by herself.

The last one to leave will be LeAnne. She's a sophomore in high school. In only two more years she'll be off to college. Mary Annie and I will become just two again, just as it was that hot August Saturday afternoon when we married. The plans we made for ourselves soon became plans for five. There were always ball games to go to, cheerleading practices, cattle judging. I make myself a promise that I'll prepare myself for this change in our lives. I'll start planning to do some of the things we wanted to do and couldn't do when the children were small. Maybe we can travel, read the books that we promised ourselves to read, go to the movies, or go camping. Or maybe we'll just sit in the two rockers on the front porch looking down the driveway for a sign that the kids might just come home.

ACKNOWLEDGMENTS

I wish to thank my editor, Laura Yorke, for her wisdom and insight. Her assistant, Lara Asher, was a tremendous resource. Beth Vesel, my agent, made this book happen, and Carole Chase was with us every step of the way. But it is the contributors themselves who deserve credit for the power and complexity of this collection.

ABOUT THE EDITOR

Christina Baker Kline is the author of two novels, *Desire Lines* and *SweetWater.* She is coauthor with Christina L. Baker of *The Conversation Begins: Mothers and Daughters Talk About Living Feminism* and editor of *Child of Mine: Original Essays on Becoming a Mother.* Her work has appeared in *The Yale Review, Ms., Parents Magazine, Southern Living, Family Life,* and *The New York Times Book Review,* among other publications. She lives in Montclair, New Jersey, with her husband, David, and two young sons, Hayden and Will.

ABOUT THE CONTRIBUTORS

Rosemary Bray, an author and editor for more than twenty years, is also a candidate for the Unitarian Universalist ministry. A former editor of *The New York Times Book Review,* Rosemary is the author of two books: *Martin Luther King,* a children's biography, and the political memoir *Unafraid of the Dark.* Her work has appeared in a variety of magazines and newspapers, including *The New York Times, Ms., Glamour, Essence, Redbook,* and the *Village Voice.* She is married to Robert McNatt, a financial writer, and is the mother of two preschool sons, Allen and Daniel.

Larry Brown's most recent novel is *Father and Son*. A past recipient of the Southern Book Critics Circle Award, Brown has published five books of fiction and one of nonfiction. He is currently working on a novel, *Wild Child*. He and his wife, Mary Annie, have three children, Billy Ray, Shane, and LeAnne, and live in Yocona, Mississippi.

Kevin Canty is the author of the story collection *A Stranger in This World* and the novels *Into the Great Wide Open* and *Nine Below Zero*. His essays and short fiction have appeared in *Esquire, The New Yorker, Vogue, Details, The New York Times,* and elsewhere. He is currently teaching at the University of Montana in Missoula, where he lives with his wife, the photographer Lucy Capehart, and their two children, Turner, nine, and Nora, five.

Maxine Chernoff has published six books of poems; two books of stories, *Bop* and *Signs of Devotion;* and two novels, *Plain Grief* and *American Heaven,* which was the 1997 runner-up for the Bay Area Book Reviewers Award in fiction. Her new novel is *Thaw.* Currently chair of creative writing at San Francisco State University, she lives in northern California with her husband, the poet, novelist, and editor Paul Hoover, and their twin thirteen-year-old sons, Julian and Philip. Their daughter, Koren, twenty-two, is in college.

Gordon Churchwell lives in Cold Spring, New York, with his wife, Julie, a graphic designer, and their two-year-old daughter, Olivia. He has written for television, magazines, and new media. He cowrote the award-winning documentary *To Know Where They Are,* about one family's experience of the Holocaust in Poland, which was shown on public television and at the Museum of Modern Art. He is currently writing a book on men's experience of pregnancy, *Pregnant Man,* which will be published by Golden Books in the fall of 1999.

Alice Elliott Dark is the author of *Naked to the Waist,* a collection of stories. Her work has appeared in *The New Yorker, Double Take, Best American Short Stories 1994,* and *Best American Short Stories of the Century.* "In the Gloaming," a story, was made into films by HBO and Trinity Playhouse. A new collection, *In the Gloaming,* and a novel will be out soon. She is a past recipient of a National Endowment for the Arts Fellowship and lives in Montclair, New Jersey, with her husband and seven-year-old son.

Tony Eprile teaches literature and writing at Bennington College and lives in Vermont with his wife, the writer Judith D. Schwartz, and their son, Brendan. He is the author of *Temporary Sojourner and Other South African Stories* and has had work published in numerous magazines, including *Ploughshares, Glimmer Train, Details,* and *George.* He has received two National Endowment for the Arts awards and is on the literature panel of the Dorland Mountain Arts Colony. His favorite collection of children's stories is *The Long Grass Whispers* by Geraldine Elliot.

Lindsay Fleming lives in Baltimore and teaches in the writing seminars at The Johns Hopkins University, from which she earned an M.A. in Fiction Writing in 1996. Her work was included in *Scribner's Best of the Fiction Workshops/1997.* She is married and has one child, Emily, age eight.

Annaliese Hood still lives in Mt. Chase, Maine, although her children—Tamara, twenty-three; Tanek, twenty-two; and Arrick, nineteen—have all stepped out into the world. A contributing writer to *Maine Times* and a columnist writing about a woman's life on a dirt road, she has published poems, essays, and short stories in *Hip Mama, Echoes, Maine in Print,* and *The Writing Self,* among other publications. Many of her essays have been broadcast on Maine Public Radio. She is also an artist working in pressed flowers, ferns, and mosses.

Hilary Selden Illick writes fiction and nonfiction. Awards for her fiction include the Michael Rubin Award for collected stories, the Herbert Wilner Short Story Award from the San Francisco State University Creative Writing MFA Program, and a National Intro Award for her short story, *Out of Body*. She has published nonfiction articles in various publications across the country, among them *The Utne Reader* and *Z Magazine,* and in newspapers and magazines in Paris, France. She lives in Berkeley, California, with her husband, Pierre, and their four children, Zoé, six, Esmé, four, and their new boy/girl twins, Nico and Téa.

Roberta Israeloff is the author of four books: *Kindling the Flame, Lost and Found, In Confidence,* and *Coming to Terms.* A contributing editor at *Parents,* she also writes about family issues for many of the women's magazines, including *Good Housekeeping, Woman's Day,* and *Redbook.* She taught writing for many years at Hunter College and New York University. She now lives in East Northport, New York, with her husband, David, a psychologist, and two sons, Jake, ten, and Ben, sixteen.

Jon Katz, the author of five novels and three nonfiction books, including *Running to the Mountain,* is a contributor to Slashdot.org (slashdot.org) and a contributing editor of *Rolling Stone*. His next nonfiction book is *The Rise of the Geeks*. He lives in Montclair, New Jersey, with his wife, Paula Span, their daughter, Emma Span, and two yellow labs, Julius and Stanley.

Michael Laser has been writing fiction for twenty-five years. He has supported himself with a variety of less-than-ideal jobs, including Good Humor man, paralegal, and word-processing temp, but has finally found a more satisfying (if hectic) balance: writing grant proposals for nonprofit organizations, serving as his children's primary caregiver, and writing fiction in every free minute. His short stories have appeared in many literary magazines. He has published a children's book, *The Rain,* and a novel, *Old Buddy Old Pal.* He and his wife, Jennifer Prost, live in Montclair, New Jersey, with their daughter, Helen, and son, Alexander.

Although born in Israel, **Yona Zeldis McDonough** was raised in Brooklyn, New York. Her most recent book, *Anne Frank,* is a biography illustrated by her mother, painter Malcah Zeldis. *Sisters in Strength: Ten American Women Who Made a Difference* is an illustrated collection of biographies for children and will be published in the year 2000. McDonough presently lives in Brooklyn with her husband, photographer Paul A. McDonough, and their two children, James, seven, and Kate, three.

Carol Muske-Dukes is a poet, novelist, essayist, and professor of English and creative writing at the University of Southern California. She has published six books of poems, including the recent *An Octave Above Thunder;* two novels, both of which have been optioned for feature films; and a collection of her critical essays and reviews, *Women and Poetry: Truth, Auto-*

biography and the Shape of the Self. She is a regular reviewer for *The New York Times Book Review, The L.A. Times Book Review,* and *The Nation.* The mother of Annie Cameron, fifteen, and stepmother to Shawn, thirty-one, she lives with her husband, actor David Dukes, and her daughter in Los Angeles.

Noelle Oxenhandler's essays have appeared in *The New Yorker, The New York Times Magazine, Vogue,* and *Tricycle,* as well as other national and literary magazines and anthologies. The mother of a thirteen-year-old daughter, Ariel, she lives in northern California where she conducts a private writing workshop. She is currently at work on a book, *The Eros of Parenthood,* to be published by Golden Books.

Richard Panek is the author of two nonfiction books, *Seeing and Believing: How the Telescope Opened Our Eyes and Minds to the Heavens* and *Waterloo Diamonds.* He is also a PEN Award–winning short story writer, and he has written for *The New York Times Magazine, Natural History, Esquire, Outside, Elle,* and *Mirabella.* He lives in New York with his wife and two sons.

Francine Prose's articles and essays have appeared in *The Atlantic, DoubleTake, The New York Times Magazine, Conde Nast Traveler, Vogue,* and *Allure.* Her most recent book is a collection of two novellas titled *Guided Tours of Hell.* Among her other books are the novels *Hunters and Gatherers, Primitive People,* and *Bigfoot Dreams.* Her short fiction has appeared in *The New Yorker, The Atlantic, The Paris Review,* and *Best American Short Stories 1991.* She lives with her husband and two sons in New York City and the Upper Hudson Valley.

Susan Fromberg Schaeffer is the author of eleven novels, five volumes of poetry, one volume of short stories, over two hundred book reviews, many scholarly articles, and two children's books. Her most recent novels are *The Golden Rope* and *The Autobiography of Foudini M. Cat*. She has won numerous awards, including two O. Henry Best Short Story Awards and a Guggenheim Fellowship, and was nominated for a National Book Award in Poetry. She was Brooklundian Professor at Brooklyn College, where she taught for twenty-eight years. She has two children and divides her time between New York and Vermont.

Jill Smolowe is the author of the memoir *An Empty Lap: One Couple's Journey to Parenthood*. An award-winning journalist, she has been on the writing staffs of *The New York Times, Newsweek, People,* and *Time*. Her work has also appeared in many other publications, including *Family Life* and *Adoptive Families*. She; her husband, Joe Treen; and their daughter, Becky, four, divide their time between Montclair, New Jersey, and Pennsylvania's Endless Mountains.

Rob Spillman is currently the book columnist for *Details*. His essays and reviews have appeared in *The Baltimore Sun, British GQ, Connoisseur, The New York Times Book Review, Premiere, Rolling Stone, Salon, Sports Illustrated, Spy, Vanity Fair,* and *Vogue,* among other places. For ten years Rob has been married to Elissa Schappell, a contributing editor at the *Paris Review* and *Vanity Fair,* where she is the "Hot Type" columnist. Together they are starting a literary magazine, *Tin House*. They live with their three-year-old daughter and newborn son in Brooklyn, New York.

Valerie Wilson Wesley is the author of *Ain't Nobody's Business If I Do* and the Tamara Hayle mystery series, which includes *When Death Comes Stealing* and *Easier to Kill*. She has written a picture book for children, *Freedom's Gifts: A Juneteenth Story*, and a young adult novel, *Where Do I Go from Here?*, for which she received an ALA Best Book for Reluctant Readers citation. She is formerly executive editor and currently a contributing editor of *Essence*, and her fiction and nonfiction have appeared in *Family Circle*, *TV Guide*, *Ms.*, and *The New York Times*, among other publications. She is married to noted screenwriter and playwright Richard Wesley and is the mother of two grown daughters.